RAPTURE

BOOKS BY JAMES D. QUIGGLE

DOCTRINAL SERIES

Biblical History

Adam and Eve, a Biography and Theology

Angelology, a True History of Angels

Essays

Biblical Essays

Biblical Essays II

Biblical Essays III

Biblical Essays IV

Marriage and Family

Marriage and Family: A Biblical Perspective

Biblical Homosexuality

A Biblical Response to Same-gender Marriage

Doctrinal and Practical Christianity

First Steps, Becoming a Follower of Jesus Christ

A Christian Catechism (With Christopher McCuin)

Thirty-Six Essentials of the Christian Faith

The Literal Hermeneutic, Explained and Illustrated

The Old Ten In the New Covenant

Christian Living and Doctrine

Counted Worthy (with Linda M. Quiggle)

Spiritual Gifts

Why Christians Should Not Tithe

Dispensational Theology

A Primer On Dispensationalism

Understanding Dispensational Theology

Covenants and Dispensations in the Scripture

Dispensational Eschatology, An Explanation and Defense of the Doctrine

Rapture

Antichrist, His Genealogy, Kingdom, and Religion

God and Man

God's Choices, Doctrines of Foreordination, Election, Predestination

God Became Incarnate

Life, Death, Eternity

Did Jesus Go To Hell?

COMMENTARY SERIES

The Old Testament

A Private Commentary on the Bible: Judges

A Private Commentary on the Book of Ruth

A Private Commentary on the Bible: Esther

A Private Commentary on the Bible: Song of Solomon

A Private Commentary on the Bible: Daniel

A Private Commentary on the Bible: Jonah

A Private Commentary on the Bible: Habakkuk

A Private Commentary on the Bible: Haggai

The New Testament

The Gospels

A Private Commentary on the Bible: Matthew's Gospel

A Private Commentary on the Bible: Mark's Gospel

A Private Commentary on the Bible: Luke 1–12

A Private Commentary on the Bible: Luke 13–24

A Private Commentary on the Bible: John 1–12

A Private Commentary on the Bible: John 13–21

Four Voices, One Testimony

Jesus Said "I Am"

The Parables and Miracles of Jesus Christ

The Passion and Resurrection of Jesus the Christ

The Christmas Story, As Told By God

Pauline Letters

A Private Commentary on the Bible: Galatians

A Private Commentary on the Bible: Ephesians

A Private Commentary on the Bible: Philippians

A Private Commentary on the Bible: Colossians

A Private Commentary on the Bible: Thessalonians

A Private Commentary on the Bible: Pastoral Letters

A Private Commentary on the Bible: Philemon

General Letters

A Private Commentary on the Book of Hebrews

A Private Commentary on the Bible: James

A Private Commentary on the Bible: 1 Peter

A Private Commentary on the Bible: 2 Peter

A Private Commentary on the Bible: John's Epistles

A Private Commentary on the Bible: Jude

Revelation

A Private Commentary on the Bible: Revelation 1–7

A Private Commentary on the Bible: Revelation 8–16

REFERENCE SERIES

Dictionary of Doctrinal Words

Translation of Select Bible Books

Old and New Testament Chronology (With David Hollingsworth)

(Also in individual volumes: Old Testament Chronology; New Testament Chronology)

TRACTS

A Human Person: Is the Unborn Life a Person?

Biblical Marriage

How Can I Know I am A Christian?

Now That I am A Christian

Thirty-Six Essentials of the Christian Faith

What is a Pastor? / Why is My Pastor Eating the Sheep?

Principles and Precepts of the Literal Hermeneutic

(All tracts are in digital format and cost $0.99)

Formats

Print, Digital, Epub. Search "James D. Quiggle" or book title.

Rapture

James D. Quiggle

A Bible Study on the
Rapture of the
New Testament Church

Copyright Page

Rapture

Copyright 2022, James D. Quiggle. All rights reserved.

ISBN: 979-8-9871044-8-4

Published by James D. Quiggle

Some of the material in this book first appeared in the following publications by James D. Quiggle.

A Private Commentary on the Bible: John's Epistles. 2016.

A Private Commentary on the Bible: Revelation 1–7. 2022.

A Private Commentary on the Bible: Thessalonians. 2021.

Biblical Essays. 2018.

Biblical Essays II. 2019.

Biblical Essays III. 2020.

Biblical Essays IV. 2021.

Dictionary of Doctrinal Words. 2018.

Dispensational Eschatology, An Explanation and Defense of the Doctrine. 2013.

Thirty-six Essentials of the Christian Faith. 2021.

For
Tilley Lee
and others looking for answers
from the Scripture

Table of Contents

Preface

For several years I have written various essays on the rapture of the New Testament church, and written commentaries on Bible books where certain scripture passages have something to say on the subject. Many people have asked me to gather that material, scattered over several books into one book. This is that book.

As often happens when much is written over several years and several books about different aspects of the same biblical subject, there is a certain amount of repetition. I have lightly edited certain material to minimize repetition.

Is the Rapture an Essential Doctrine?

What is an essential doctrine of the New Testament church?

An essential doctrine of the Christian faith is a fundamental truth drawn solely from the sixty-six canonical books of Scripture, the denial or absence of which does not conform to the biblical and apostolic Christian faith as it is expressed and defined by the Scripture.

A simpler definition for popular use is, "a doctrine of Scripture which, when missing or denied, Christianity ceases to be the Christianity defined and exampled in the Scripture."

The rapture of the New Testament church is a fact revealed in Scripture, and therefore it is a doctrine of the New Testament church. The rapture as an essential doctrine may be stated like this:

Jesus the Christ is returning to the air to remove his New Testament church from the earth.

Is the rapture an advent of deity? No. Zechariah 14:4 defines an advent of deity: feet on the ground. "And his [YHWH, 14:3] feet will stand in that day [second advent] on the Mount of Olives."

The first advent set the pattern for an advent of deity: feet on the ground.

Luke 1:31, Look now, you will conceive in your womb, and will bear a son, and you will call his name "Jesus."

Luke 2:7, And she birthed her son, the firstborn, and swaddled him, and laid him in a barn, because there was not a place for them in the lodging.

Luke 2:11–12, For to you has been born today a savior, who is Christ the Lord. And this to you the sign: you will find a baby, swaddled, and lying in a barn."

Only the second advent, Zechariah 14:4, meets the pattern for an advent of deity as set by the first advent. The rapture is not an advent because it is defined as meeting Christ "in the air," 1 Thessalonians 4:17, not on the ground.

Then we the living remaining, together with them, will be caught up in the clouds for the meeting of the Lord in the air.

There is a return of the Lord to the air for his New Testament church, and a return to the earth at a later time which is the second advent.

The rapture is a fact. The rapture is not an advent. The rapture is not part of the second advent. The rapture is an essential doctrine of the New Testament church.

The doctrine of the rapture of the New Testament church is based on the promise Jesus made to the New Testament church at John 14:2–3, "In my Father's house are many abiding places; but if not I would have said that to you. I go to prepare a place for you. And when I should go and prepare a place for you, I am coming again and will receive you to myself; that where I am, you may be also."

The timing of the rapture, whether one believes it to be pre-tribulation, mid-tribulation, or post-tribulation, is not an essential doctrine. Let me repeat: the timing of the rapture of the New Testament church is not part of the essential doctrine of the rapture. Those who make timing an essential doctrine create unlawful divisions in the church.

The partial rapture theory is not a biblical doctrine, but is heretical. In the partial rapture view theory believers are raptured when they become worthy: some before the Tribulation; others during the Tribulation; and still others endure the entire Tribulation. This theory denies Christ propitiated God for sin.

If, as is the case, Christ propitiated—completely and fully satisfied—God's holiness and justice for the believer's sin, 1 John 2:2, and Christ is the believer's Advocate before the Father, 1 John 2:1, and the believer's high priest who intercedes for the believer, Hebrews 7:25, and has made the believer righteous, 2 Corinthians 5:21, and sanctified the believer, Hebrews 10:14, then any one believer is as worthy as any other believer to be raptured when Christ returns to the air to catch away his church to heaven.

What is the Rapture?

The English word "rapture" is a transliteration of (a grammatical form of) the Latin word *rapiō*, which in English means "caught up." This Latin word was used in the Vulgate (Latin) version of 1 Thessalonians 4:17 to translate the Greek word *harpázō* [Zodhiates, s. v. 726], which in English means "caught up."

> Then we the living remaining, together with them, will be *harpázō* in the clouds for the meeting of the Lord in the air.

This word *harpázō* is used thirteen times in the New Testament. The use at Acts 8:39–40 illustrates the meaning: "Now when they came up out of the water, the Spirit of the Lord *harpázō* (caught up) Philip, and the eunuch saw him no more; for he went on his way rejoicing. But Philip was found at Azotus." Compare 2 Corinthians 12:2, "*harpázō* such a one to the third heaven" and 12:4, "*harpázō* into the paradise."

The *harpázō* of the New Testament church is a yet-future event when physically living believers will be transformed and glorified, and then caught up into the air at the command of Christ, to be taken away from earth into the spirit domain to live with Christ endlessly in the immediate presence of God.

(The immediate or effective presence of God is not his omnipresence but God positively interacting with sinners to save them, and interacting with his saved people to conform them to the image of their Savior Jesus Christ, and bring them home to heaven sinless, transformed, glorified, at the designated end of their mortal live, to live endlessly in his active presence. God's active presence is the privilege of those few who will have or do have a salvific relationship with God.)

Raptured believers will not experience physical death. At the moment of being caught up, both body and soul of the physically living believer will be glorified to be free from the presence of sin, and both body and soul will be transformed to be incorruptible, and will live endlessly in the immediate presence of God in that incorruptible state.

Definition: The rapture is the bodily return of Christ to the air for his New Testament church, to resurrect the dead in Christ, to transform the living and the resurrected to be fit for God's presence, to call the transformed church up to himself in the air, and to take the church to heaven, John 14:2–3; 1 Thessalonians 4:13–18.

The discerning reader will have noticed no mention is made of timing. Although I have strong opinions concerning the timing of the rapture of the New Testament church, the timing is not essential to the doctrine. To break fellowship over differences in opinion as to the timing of the rapture is wrong.

The following is an in depth discussion of the rapture of the New Testament church. The discussion may seem far-ranging, but many other doctrines interact with the doctrine of the rapture.

What Jesus Said

Without question Jesus Christ is returning to the earth. Not spiritually or in some sort of manifestation, but physically, bodily, literally. His return is so clear all biblically based theologies teach he is returning.

> John 14:2–3, In my Father's house are many abiding places; but if not I would have said that to you. I go to prepare a place for you. And when I should go and prepare a place for you, I am coming again and will receive you to myself; that where I am, you may be also.

> Luke 21:25–28, And there will be signs in the sun and moon and stars. And on the earth anguish of nations in perplexity, roaring of the sea and rolling billows, people faint of heart from fear and expectation of that which is coming on the earth. For the powers of the heavens will be shaken. And then they will see the Son of Man coming in a cloud, with power and great glory. Now these things beginning to happen, look up and lift up your heads, because your redemption draws near.

The question is not the fact of Christ's return, but the character and timing of his return. If one collates the testimony of the Synoptic Gospels concerning Christ's return, and compares that with John's Gospel concerning the return, one will discover that the Synoptics associate Christ's return with the Tribulation, but in John's Gospel Christ's return is not associated with the Tribulation. Put simply, the focus of the eschatological passages in the Synoptics is Israel, the Tribulation, the Second Advent, and the Davidic-Messianic Kingdom. The focus of the eschatological passage in John's Gospel is the rapture/resurrection of the New Testament church.

The Synoptics' Witness of Jesus' Return

In the Synoptic gospels Jesus speaks of an "abomination of desolation," which he links to the same topic in Daniel's prophecies, Daniel 9:27; Matthew 24:15; Mark 13:14. In the Synoptics Jesus speaks of a time of great tribulation so severe that unless the duration of it was shortened by the Lord none could be saved from physical death, Matthew 25:21–22; Mark 13:19–20. During that time of great tribulation false prophets will arise to deceive the world, the sun will become darkened, the moon will be dimmed, and stars will fall from heaven; then the sign of Christ's return will be seen in the heavens, Matthew 25:29–30; Mark 13:24–26; Luke 21:25–28. At his return Jesus will send his angels to gather his elect from throughout the earth, Matthew 25:31; Mark 13:27.

John's Gospel says nothing about Tribulation events. Of importance then is that word in John from Jesus, "I . . . will receive you to myself," which is not the same as sending his angels to gather his elect.

In Matthew 24:9, Mark 13:9, and Luke 21:12 Jesus speaks of his disciples being persecuted, but rescued, Matthew 24:13, 31; Mark 13:13, 27; Luke 21:28. John's Gospel speaks of Christians being scattered and killed after the Lord has ascended, John 16:2, 32, but in these verses Jesus does not speak of returning to rescue them from their troubles.

In John's gospel the church follows Jesus into the world, 21:19, 22, where it will face persecution, 15:18–20; 16:33; 17:14–15. The ending of John's Gospel tells the New Testament church what it is to do in the interim between Christ's ascension and his return for the church: follow him. The ending of John's Gospel is a deliberate contrast with the closing scenes of the Synoptics and opening scene of the book of Acts (which agrees with the Synoptic view of eschatology). In the Synoptics and Acts Jesus says he will return with power and glory to receive the kingdom promised to David, Luke 21:27; Acts 1:6; 2 Samuel 7:12–17; Psalm 2.

In John's gospel believers are to be in the world following Jesus until he returns to receive them unto himself. In contrast the believers spoken of in the eschatological passages in the Synoptics are to wait for deliverance: "by your endurance you will possess your souls," Luke

21:19; "Now the one having endured to the end, he will be delivered," Mark 13:13; "look up and lift up your heads, because your redemption draws near," Luke 21:28. These words are spoken in the context of great Tribulation.

The apostles' question at Acts 1:6, "Lord, if at this time, are you restoring the kingdom to Israel?" connects with their questions in the Synoptics, "What is the sign of your coming; and the completion of the age?" The Jews knew from Old Testament prophecy that the consummation or completion of the age was the ending of the current age in which Israel was under gentile domination, Luke 21:24, and the beginning of the Messianic kingdom when Christ brought Israel salvation from their enemies and Israel ruled the gentiles. None of this is in John's Gospel.

At Jesus' ascension in Acts 1 the disciples were looking for something other, something more than, being with Jesus (John 14:3). They were looking for the Davidic-Messianic Kingdom, not the home Jesus was going to heaven to prepare for them, John 14:2. To be fair to the disciples they felt Jesus had set the stage for their question about the kingdom with the announcement they would receive the Holy Spirit. The Holy Spirit was to be "poured out" to the Jews when the kingdom was inaugurated. See, for example, Isaiah 32:15; 44:3; Joel 2:28–29; Zechariah 10:10. Jesus' response in Acts 1:7–8 put aside the question of the kingdom, and by 2:16 Peter had worked out what Jesus was saying about the Holy Spirit. Jesus revealed to Paul the details of his return for his church, and that makes sense, because Paul was apostle to the gentiles—the New Testament church is predominantly saved gentiles—thus separating Jesus' return for his church from his answer to the disciples about his return for Israel and its Davidic-Messianic Kingdom.

The differing characteristics of Christ's return between John and the Synoptics indicates the Synoptic view of eschatology concerns Israel only, i.e., national ethnic Israel, but John's Gospel looks only to the New Testament church. The questions the apostles (Mark 13:3) asked at Matthew 24:3 (and parallel verses in Mark and Luke) that resulted in the discourse about coming tribulation and Christ's return were strictly interested in the future of national ethnic Israel. These were their questions.

When will these things be?

What will be the sign of your coming?

What will be the sign of the end of the age?

To understand Jesus' answers to these questions, we must understand the context in which they were asked and answered. The immediate subject was the temple, the essential component of Judaism, which would be present during the Davidic-Messianic Kingdom, Ezekiel 40–48. Who was Jesus? The Messiah. What was the occasion? A prediction that Judaism as they knew it would be destroyed (because the temple would be destroyed). Who were the questioners? Jewish men looking for the Jewish Davidic-Messianic Kingdom and believing Jesus was the Jewish Messiah of that Jewish kingdom. What were the men expecting? Jesus the Jewish Messiah to judge his enemies, cleanse national ethnic Israel, subject the gentiles to Israel's rule, and by these actions bring the Jewish Davidic-Messianic Kingdom into existence—soon.

So the context is Jewish men were asking the man they believed to be the Jewish Messiah questions about the Jewish Davidic-Messianic Kingdom. Those Jewish men asked those questions of the Jewish Messiah because the Jewish Messiah had just told them the Jewish temple would be destroyed, and these men knew from the Jewish prophet Ezekiel that in the Jewish Davidic-Messianic Kingdom there would be a new Jewish temple.

The context is national ethnic Israel and Messianic prophecies given to national ethnic Israel, to be fulfilled for national ethnic Israel, not the New Testament church, and we should not seek to force the New Testament church into the Synoptic gospel passages.

The answers Jesus gave to their three questions did not relate to the New Testament church. These men were concerned with Israel. Jesus answered them as an Israeli speaking to Israelis concerned with Israel. Every prophesied event in Jesus' end-times discourse in Matthew, Mark, and Luke concerned Israel, not the New Testament church.

Gospel of John's Witness of Jesus' Return

In contrast, John's Gospel is all about the New Testament church. That gospel's message is believe Jesus of Nazareth is the Christ, the

Son of God, and in believing be saved and have eternal life in his name, John 20:31. John ends his gospel with the disciples following Jesus: working while waiting for Jesus to return for them.

In John's gospel there is no mention of Tribulation preceding Jesus' return, as there is in the Synoptic gospels. In John 20:22 Jesus said to Peter (paraphrasing), "If I want John to remain on the earth until I return, how does that affect your mission? You follow me." And so the New Testament church—every person saved from Christ's resurrection until the rapture—will remain on earth serving Jesus until he returns; Returns for the New Testament church, 1 Thessalonians 4:13–18; 1 Corinthians 15:51–52; 2 Thessalonians 2:1. Not return after great Tribulation with the "power and glory" necessary to receive his Davidic-Messianic Kingdom, but return before the Tribulation (discussed later) to receive his church unto himself.

In the upper room discourse, Jesus told them, John 14:2, that in heaven ("my Father's house") there were many places to live. Jesus told them he was going to heaven to prepare those places for them. Therefore, when he told them he would return to receive them to himself, in order for them to be with him, the meaning must be that he was returning to take them to heaven to those dwelling places he had prepared.

Jesus' statements at John 14:2–3 conflict with his statements in the Synoptics if one views his return in John to be the same as his return in the Synoptics. In John, Jesus is returning to take a redeemed people to heaven to be with him. In the Synoptics when he returns he is bringing redemption with him, Luke 21:28, Mark 13:13. When Jesus returns for his church he himself will receive them, John 14:3. When he returns in the Synoptics the angels will gather his elect out of the world where God scattered them. Israel was scattered, 722 BC, 606 BC, and AD 70, and despite the creation of a Jewish nation in AD 1948 much of Israel is still scattered, In 1948 Christ did not send his angels to gather national ethnic Israel to a nation newly formed by a United Nations resolution, not by the King's return.

The New Testament church is not scattered throughout the world, it is a people saved out of the world, out of every nation, tribe, people, and tongue. There are no outward signs marking Jesus' return for his church, John 14:3. There are many outward signs when he returns in the Synoptics, Matthew 25:29–30; Mark 13:24–26; Luke 21:25–28. The angels in Acts 1:11 said when Jesus returned to restore the kingdom, Acts 1:6, it would be in like manner as he went into heaven, which is described at 1:9, with clouds, to the earth. John says nothing about clouds. Nothing Jesus said about his return for the church in John 14:2–3 corresponds with the Synoptics' and Acts' characterization of his return.

Two Returns, One Advent

The differing character of Jesus' return between the Synoptics and John's Gospel suggests a difference in timing and purpose. The dispensationalist's insistence on a literal hermeneutic discovers God has a separate purpose for national ethnic Israel and the New Testament church, resulting in different plans and processes of eschatology. When one compares the two accounts of the Lord's return—the Synoptics and John—one comes to the conclusion that the purpose and timing of one is not the same as the purpose and timing of the other. That they are in fact two separate events: one for the New Testament church and one for national ethnic Israel.

The two separate returns are not two advents. The advent of deity is characterized by Jesus' first advent: deity incarnate in humanity, feet-on-the-ground, literally, physically, bodily present on the physical surface of the earth. The second advent is so identified in Zechariah 14:3, 4. "Then YHWH will go forth . . . that day his feet will stand on the Mount of Olives . . . and the Mount of Olives will be split [in the] middle." But at Jesus' return for the church he is in the air, 1 Thessalonians 4:17, "we the living [with the resurrected saints] . . . will be caught up in clouds for a meeting of the Lord in the air." There will be a return in the air for the New Testament church, and a separate return to the earth to receive the Davidic-Messianic Kingdom. Two distinct returns: to the air to rapture the New Testament church before the second advent; the return to the earth that is the second advent.

The dispensational view of two distinct returns is shared by others who would claim themselves non-dispensational. Most dispensationalists locate Jesus' return for the church prior to the beginning of the Tribulation period that is described in the Old Testament (the "Day of the Lord"), in the Synoptics, and in Revelation 6–19. This is known as the pretribulational rapture.

Others locate Jesus' return for the church at the middle of the Tribulation (midtribulational or pre-wrath rapture) or at the end of the Tribulation (posttribulational rapture) thus recognizing a separate return for the church in the air. In the posttribulational view the return for the church is combined with the second advent: Jesus calls the church up as he is coming down at the second advent.

Dispensational eschatology is distinct in placing the return for the church before the Tribulation. That is because the Tribulation period is one of those "plans and processes" (the Day of the Lord) which God has designed particularly for national ethnic Israel, not the New Testament church. The point to be made is that dispensationalism is not alone in understanding two returns, first for the church and then for Israel, even if the timing is different.

The Character Of The Rapture Of The Church

Having established that Jesus taught two events comprising his return, one event that is the rapture, one event that is the advent, let us (in keeping with the theme of this book) examine his return to the air for the church. We will begin with the character of the rapture and then discuss what I believe to be its timing.

Jesus' return for the church is known in dispensational eschatology as the rapture of the church which takes place before the Day of the Lord, aka the great Tribulation. The word "rapture" is from the Latin *rapio*, to snatch to oneself, to seize hastily, used in the Latin (Vulgate) version to translate the Greek word *hárpazō* in 1 Thessalonians 4:17, "to snatch away," which most versions translate "caught up."

> Then we the living, remaining together with them [the resurrected], will be *hárpazō* in the clouds for a meeting of the Lord in the air, and so always with the Lord we will be.

There are important details in 4:16, which I will combine with 4:17.

> 16 Because the Lord himself, by a loud command, by the voice of an archangel, and by the trumpet of God, will descend from heaven, and the dead in Christ will rise first. 17 Then we the living remaining, together with them, will be caught up in the clouds for the meeting of the Lord in the air. And so always with the Lord we will be.

The word translated "air" in 4:17, is the Greek word *aḗr* [Zodhiates. s. v. 109]. The Jews conceived of the *aḗr* as a spirit domain where Satan and his angels lived. The Greeks understood *aḗr* to be a kind of atmosphere that filled the space between the earth and the moon, beyond which was heaven, the abode of higher spirits. Thus in both religions the *aḗr* was the abode of the lower spirits.

In biblical use *aḗr* sometimes means earth's atmosphere, e.g., Acts 22:23; Revelation 9:2, and sometimes the spirit domain, e.g., Ephesians 2:2. (All uses: those mentioned plus 1 Corinthians 9:26; 14:9; Revelation 16:17.) Paul is not conforming to either Jewish or Greek cosmology, but is using and redefining a familiar term to communicate spiritual truth.

The meaning of *aḗr* in 1 Thessalonians 4:17 could be earth's atmosphere or the spirit domain. Because the rapture calls the saved to come to the "many abiding places" in "my Father's house" (John 14:2), a dual meaning is not improper: up into the atmosphere to meet the Lord, then on to the spirit domain third heaven where believers will live for eternity. The church is called up into the first heaven, the sky ("in clouds"), to meet the Lord, to be taken to "my Father's house," the third heaven, a location in the spirit domain where God has a permanent manifestation of his presence, Revelation 4.

The other possibility is clouds refer to the angels accompanying the Lord, the church is caught up into the second spirit domain heaven to meet the Lord, and then the church is taken to the third heaven in the spirit domain.

(The Bible speaks of three heavens. A first heaven, which is where we live: the atmospheric sky and the starry sky. A second heaven, the spirit domain where angels live. Genesis 22:15; 28:12; Romans 10:6; Revelation 5:11. A third heaven because Paul states he was there, 2 Corinthians 12:2. Paul calls the third heaven paradise. He received visions and revelations there.)

There is a valid reason for suspecting the "clouds" in 1 Thessalonians 4:17 are angels in the spirit domain's second and third heavens. The Scripture reveals there is an archangel with angels under his authority that watch over national ethnic Israel, Daniel 12:1; Revelation 12:7. The archangel Michael is only found in Scripture in connection with national ethnic Israel. Therefore it is rational the archangel of 1 Thessalonians 4:16 is not Michael the archangel, but an unknown archangel, revealed in 4:16, that with angels under his authority watch over the New Testament church. How fitting they should accompany the Lord when he comes to rapture his New Testament church.

We know from Paul's second letter, 2 Thessalonians 2:15, that Paul had explained these things concerning the rapture, 1 Thessalonians 4:13–18, in person during his short visit, Acts 17. Although we may interpret the exact meaning of *aér* to the best of our ability, the Thessalonian church, composed of Jews and gentiles, knew exactly what Paul meant by meeting the Lord in the *aér*.

In the chronological order biblical scholars believe Paul's letters were written, 1 Thessalonians was the first letter, and 2 Thessalonians the second. In 2:1 of the second letter Paul assured the Thessalonians the rapture had not already come by writing of the coming as a yet-future event.

> Now we implore you, brethren, by the coming of our Lord Jesus Christ and our gathering together unto him.

Paul continued and said the Thessalonians were not to be shaken in mind or troubled as though the rapture had already come, v. 2, because the *apostasía* (departure) must come first and the "man of *anomía* (lawlessness)" revealed, v. 3. The rapture comes before the Tribulation period, because the man of lawlessness, the Antichrist, is revealed during the Tribulation. (I will discuss *apostasía* in chapter "Second Thessalonians 2:1–3.")

Paul's last mention of the rapture is at 1 Corinthians 15:51–53.

> Behold, something hidden I tell to you. We will not all sleep, but we will all be changed, in an instant, in the twinkling of an eye, at the last trumpet. For the trumpet will announce, and the dead ones will be raised incorruptible, and we will be transformed. For it is necessary this the corruptible to put on incorruption, and this the mortal to put on immortality.

"Sleep" is a biblical euphemism for physical death. The "twinkling" of an eye is a colorful figure of speech meaning in a moment, in an instant.

All the information Paul gives about the rapture (1 Thessalonians

4:16–17; 2 Thessalonians 2:1; 1 Corinthians 15:51–53) may be combined to completely describe the rapture event.

> In regard to the coming of our Lord Jesus Christ and our gathering together unto him, behold, something hidden I tell to you. We will not all sleep, but we will all be changed. Because the Lord himself—by a loud command, by the voice of an archangel, in an instant, in the twinkling of an eye, and by the trumpet of God, at the last trumpet—for the trumpet will announce, and the dead in Christ will rise up first, and the dead ones will be raised incorruptible. Then we the living remaining, together with them, will be transformed. For it is necessary this the corruptible to put on incorruption, and this the mortal to put on immortality. And we all will be caught up in the clouds for the meeting of the Lord in the air. And so always with the Lord we will be.

When the applicable scriptures are brought together we see that what Paul said concerning the rapture presents a complete and understandable testimony consistent with John 14:2–3: Jesus is returning to receive his church to himself.

It is significant these verses do not mention Israel. The context in which these verses were written is a New Testament letter written by a New Testament apostle to New Testament believers, i.e., the New Testament church. The only way to find the "New Israel" of Reformed theology in these verses is to import the idea.

At an unknown and unknowable date in the future, a date not preceded by any signs to let us know it is coming, Jesus will return to receive his church unto himself. He will first call the physically dead saints to resurrection. Naturally this means he will bring the souls of those physically dead saints with him, 1 Thessalonians 4:14, "Because if we believe that Jesus died and rose again, so also God will bring with him those having fallen asleep through Jesus." The purpose of resurrection is to re-form (resurrect) the bodies of the physically dead saints and reunite their souls to their bodies. Those souls that died in Christ were transformed in their physical death to be sinless, and their resurrected bodies will be re-formed without sin; in Paul's words, "raised incorruptible."

At about the same time the resurrection-reunification is happening for those who died in Jesus, living believers are being glorified and transformed. These are separate but near-simultaneous events. The living saints are glorified when their souls are cleansed from sin, becoming incorruptible. At the same instant their bodies are transformed, i.e., cleansed from sin to become incorruptible.

These events happening to the living and to the resurrected saints are completed before the echo of Jesus' shout, the archangel's voice, and the sounding of the trumpet fades away. Then the resurrected and the living saints will be transported to the third heaven spirit domain to be always with the Lord, even as he said, John 14:3, and even as he prayed, John 17:24.

Above I said there were no signs to let the church know when the rapture would take place. I will discuss this subject below. Here let us notice that if "It is not yours to know the times or seasons which the Father has placed in his own authority," Acts 1:7, then we cannot know when the rapture will take place. Looking for so-called "signs of the times" that are supposed to let the church known the rapture is near contradicts Scripture. That word from Jesus in Acts 1:7 concerned the Davidic-Messianic Kingdom, but if the timing of the kingdom is known, then an approximate date for the rapture can be set, because the rapture is about seven years before the second advent.

The Timing Of The Rapture Of The Church

I will emphasize again the timing of the rapture is not an essential doctrine of the New Testament church. Differences are *not* a reason to break fellowship. But naturally I have an opinion, and I would not be true to my calling as a Bible teacher if I did not introduce you to that opinion. My work here is not to change your mind—that is the Holy Spirit's job—but only to explain how I understand the Scripture.

The Principle Of Deliverance

There is a principle in the Bible, often unnoticed, that God tends to deliver his saved people from his judgments on the worldling. Not from judgments that fall out from God's use of natural means. The sun rises and the rain falls on the just and unjust. Believers and unbelievers alike suffered in the three and one-half years of drought in Ahab's reign, 1 Kings 17:1 (cf. James 5:17). Floods, hurricanes, tornados, earthquakes, etc., fall on believers and unbelievers alike. Many times these are not judgments from God but the normal course of circumstances: life happens. It is how God's saved people react during those times that establishes or makes shipwreck their testimony.

The Scripture clearly reveals that God delivers his people from those general types of judgment he brings against the world. The first of these is the Noahic Flood. God gave Noah, and the world he preached to, at least one hundred years before the worldwide flood. Noah was five hundred years old before Shem was born, Genesis 5:32; six hundred when the flood began, 7:6; Shem was one hundred years old two years after the flood, 10:10.

We see, then, that one hundred years before the flood, God came to righteous Noah, and told Noah to prepare an escape from worldwide judgment, and through Noah God proclaimed that escape to the world, 1 Peter 3:19–20. One cannot say Noah endured God's judgment against the world, because he was safe from judgment in the Ark: Noah and seven others lived; all other human beings died.

Lot was removed from Sodom before it was destroyed by God, Genesis 19:22, based on the principle Abraham spoke, 18:25, God does not slay the righteous with the wicked. Notice that the destruction of Sodom, like the Noahic Flood, was by direct action from God, Genesis 19:24, not the result of a natural disaster. Lot and two of his daughters were rescued from the judgment that killed all others in the plains of Sodom and Gomorrah.

God says in Isaiah 57:1, "The righteous die, and no one pays attention, and the merciful are taken away, none considering the righteous has been taken away from the evil to come." But in 57:21 God says there is no peace for the wicked. Jesus advised Christians to flee Jerusalem from the destruction to come, Luke 21:20–21. Tradition says the Christians in the city fled when they knew the Roman armies were on their way to besiege and destroy it.

From time to time the righteous do suffer the effects of God's wrath. When Elijah prayed and it did not rain for three and one-half years, 1 Kings 17:1; Luke 4:25; James 5:17, the righteous (7,000 persons, 1 Kings 19:18) suffered the same drought as the unrighteous. But God helped the righteous bear through the time of trouble, so for them it was not penal but circumstantial. For the unrighteous the drought was penal, and they received no help from God. Can we doubt that some of the righteous were removed before the drought, on the principle expressed at Isaiah 57:1? But some of the righteous, 7,000 persons, some perhaps saved during the drought, with God's help endured the circumstances associated with God's wrath on the unrighteous.

What about the New Testament church and the Tribulation-Day of the Lord? In 1 Thessalonians 5:4 Paul tells those Christians that the Day of the Lord (v. 1) will not overtake them. The phrase "Day of the Lord," occurring twenty-six times in the Old Testament, three in the New Testament, is the time of God's wrath against sinners during the Tribulation period. In 1 Thessalonians 5:9 Paul tells the Thessalonians that God has not appointed his saved people to his wrath, "but for obtaining deliverance through our Lord Jesus Christ." The "wrath" is God's wrath against sinners during the Day of the Lord-Tribulation.

In 5:9, Paul is speaking to saved people. Therefore the word most translate "salvation," *sōtēría* [Zodhiates, s. v. 4991], which means "safety, deliverance, preservation from danger or destruction" is better translated "deliverance."

Paul's point is simple: saved people do not endure God's wrath because Jesus will deliver them from the time of God's wrath. The New Testament church does not endure the Tribulation but is removed from that time of God's wrath by the rapture, described a few verses earlier.

But those who are unsaved when the Tribulation begins will endure God's wrath, unless they find faith and become saved. And when they do God will make a way for those Tribulation believers to bear through the circumstances; sometimes that way will be a martyrs' death, to remove them from further persecution to heavenly bliss, on the principle expressed at Isaiah 57:1.

As to the New Testament believer, the rapture of the church prevents believers of the New Testament church dispensation from suffering the wrath of God against the world in the Day of the Lord. Descriptions of the Day of the Lord in Joel clearly identify it with the Tribulation period, e.g., Joel 2:10–11, 30–31. In 1 Thessalonians 5:9 Paul said the New Testament church will not go through the Tribulation period.

What Jesus Said At Revelation 3:10

Jesus also said the New Testament church would not go through the Tribulation period. At Revelation 3:10 Jesus said to the believers of the local church at Philadelphia, Because you have kept the word of my endurance as to circumstances, I also will keep you out of the hour of the trial that is about to come upon the whole inhabited earth, to test the earth dwellers."

That Greek preposition, *ek* [Zodhiates, s. v. 1537], which I have translated "out of," but which other versions translate "from," means "out of, separated from." It is the direct opposite of the preposition *eis* [Zodhiates, s. v. 1519], which means into or in. The Philadelphian church will be kept completely separated from "the hour of the trial." Note that the Greek text reads *tas hŏra*, the hour, and *tas peirasmós*, the trial. In Greek grammar the definite article indicates specificity. Jesus is speaking of a specific period of time, a specific trial. More on this later.

The seven letters to seven churches in Revelation were intended for those churches and for all churches like them from John's apostolic time to the end of the New Testament church dispensation. Jesus told John to write about "the things which are": the church dispensation. Then he was to write about "the things which will take place after this": the Tribulation, second advent, Davidic-Millennial Kingdom, Great White Throne judgment, and the new heaven and earth. The seven letters are intended for all the churches that exist or will exist during the time of "the things which are."

The conditions detailed by Christ in each church are repeatedly discovered in local churches throughout the history of the church. His warnings, exhortations, and promises are applicable to any believer during the New Testament church dispensation. Any church at any year, month, and day during the church's history between Christ's resurrection and the rapture can be an Ephesian, Smyrnian, Pergamos, Thyatira, Sardis, Philadelphia, or Laodicean type of church—sometimes more than one type within the history of a local church!

Therefore, this word to the Philadelphians is for New Testament churches throughout the dispensation. Christ's return for the rapture is always imminent (can occur at any moment), therefore this word was applicable to any church in any generation from Christ's resurrection to the rapture. When combined with other assurances, such as discussed above in 1 Thessalonians 5:4, 9, one discovers the New Testament church living at the time just prior to "the hour of the trial," i.e., the Tribulation period, will be kept out of that hour of trial.

Is "the hour of the trial" the Tribulation period? Jesus defines "the hour" as "the trial which is about to come upon the whole habitable world to try the earth-dwellers." The term "habitable world" is *oikouménē* [Zodhiates, s. v. 3625], the earth viewed as inhabited by humankind. In the book of Revelation the term "earth-dwellers," is literally "them that dwell upon the earth" and in every use in the Revelation means those of no-faith, those who reject God and Jesus as Savior. As a figure of speech "earth-dwellers" means physically alive, spiritually dead unsaved men and women. This hour of trial, the Tribulation period, which will come upon unbelieving humankind, the earth-dwellers, is the same as the Day of the Lord.

The Day of the Lord will come upon everything proud and lofty, Isaiah 2:12. That day will leave the land desolate, and sinners will be destroyed, Isaiah 13:6. Multitudes will be saved, Joel 2:32 (cf. Revelation 7:9–17), but many more will be slain, Joel 3:14 (cf. Revelation 19:11–21). It will be an hour of darkened sun and moon, signs in the sun and moon and stars; and upon the earth distress of nations, men fainting for fear, and the powers of the heavens shall be shaken (Luke 21:26–26), earthquakes, heavens trembling, sun and moon growing dark, brightness of the stars diminished (Joel 2:10), blood and fire and pillars of smoke (Joel 2:30). These descriptions conform to what the Revelation says about the Tribulation, compare Revelation 6–19.

So there is a promise to the Philadelphian church and the Thessalonian church that those believers will be kept out of the Tribulation Period. Paul tells the Thessalonians, 2 Thessalonians 2:1–3, that they were not enduring the Tribulation. History does not record a Tribulation period occurring between Paul's Thessalonian letter, circa AD 53, to the present date. The Tribulation certainly did not occur during the lifetime of the Thessalonians and Philadelphians, something the Holy Spirit knew beforehand when he inspired those scriptures. Therefore those scriptures were intended to comfort both then-present and yet-future believers.

Aren't all the New Testament letters intended by the Holy Spirit for all believers throughout the New Testament church dispensation? If the answer is yes, then the answer is also yes for the eschatological parts of those letters. Why would the Holy Spirit give an exhortation from Paul in AD 53 (2 Thessalonians 2:1–4), and from Jesus (through John) in AD 95 (Revelation 3:10), concerning an eschatological event that was far-future to them and remains yet-future to the current generation of New Testament believers? Because the rapture is always imminent, capable of occurring at any moment. Every Christian, from first generation to last, needs the assurance they will be delivered from God's wrath on the world in the coming Day of the Lord, because it could begin at any moment.

Is not every commendation, exhortation, and promise in each of the seven Revelation letters applicable to any Christian in any time and place during the New Testament church dispensation? Yes. Even so, the word to Philadelphia concerning deliverance out of the Tribulation period applies to every generation of New Testament believers. All New Testament church dispensation believers are waiting for the at-any-moment rapture, and are assured it will happen before the Day of the Lord. Physically living believers will be kept out of the Tribulation by the rapture. Let us examine the promise to Philadelphia in detail.

Revelation 3:10 In More Detail

This promise to the Philadelphia church is a promise to those who persevere in the faith. The promise is to keep this church out of the hour of the trial. The word "hour" as used in this context does not mean a period of time as to duration, but indicates a definite event: the definite article is used, *tas hŏra*, "the hour." For example, the "hour of incense," at Luke 1:10 was a specific event occurring the same time every day (about the "ninth hour," approximately 3:00 p.m.). In Revelation 14:7 the "hour" of God's judgment on Babylon is that particular moment in time when God will execute judgment upon all that Babylon symbolizes in the Revelation. In Revelation 3:10 the reference is to a specific trial that will take place at a determined moment that is yet future in the perspective of the Philadelphians.

The time of trial is an event that will test those who "dwell on the earth," a phrase in Revelation (3:10; 6:10; 11:10; 13:8, 14; 14:6; 17:8) that always means the unsaved. The word translated "test" is *peirasmós* [Zodhiates, s. v. 3986], literally testing, and in this context does not refer to temptation but to a test or trial. The purpose of a trial is to determine the true character of those being tested. The issue to be tested concerns one's relationship to God in Christ: faith in or rejection of Christ. The matter of testing has been established in 3:8–9: to keep Jesus' commandments and name. In the context of "those who dwell on the earth," the desired outcome of the test is to respond positively to the commandment to believe on him as Savior and Lord. This is not a period of testing for believers. The believer has already faced his or her test and has chosen faith in Jesus as Savior.

For the believer, a *peirasmós* (or a *thlípsis*, affliction, tribulation, Zodhiates, s. v. 2347) is a difficulty or impediment to the outworking of faith (2 Corinthians 8:2; Galatians 4:14; Hebrews 3:8; 11:36; 1 Peter 4:12), intended to mature faith. But for the unbeliever a *peirasmós* or a *thlípsis* looks to a specific result: acquittal of guilt or guilty of sin as charged. In New Testament terms, acquittal means saved by grace through faith unto eternal life. A finding of "guilty" means unsaved and punished by the second, eternal death, Revelation 20:11–15. In Revelation 3:10 the hour of the trial (*peirasmós*) is for the unsaved during the Tribulation period (*thlípsis*) to give them that opportunity to believe, or not believe, on Jesus Christ as Savior. Many believe, Revelation 7:9–17; many more do not, Revelation 14:9–11, 17–20.

There has not been, to date, a trial to test every inhabitant upon the world in relationship to guilt or salvation concerning faith in Jesus. One might interpret the trial in a non-literal fashion as the continuing question every unsaved sinner faces: to believe on or reject Jesus as Savior. However, in a book that prophesies future judgment upon the whole earth, it seems more reasonable to understand "the hour of the trial" as referring to that future trial described in Revelation 6–19, the result of which is faith or no faith, eternal life or endless perdition.

There was no fulfillment of this prophecy in the history of the Philadelphian church, and there has not been an historical event that has tested all humankind (*oikouménē*, the world viewed as inhabited by humankind) at one time, as 3:10 indicates. Therefore, the hour of the trial in Revelation 3:10 is the Day of the Lord, the Tribulation period. The New Testament church will be kept out of the Tribulation. The promise goes well beyond fulfillment for the circa AD 95 Philadelphian church. Fulfillment of the promise is delayed until the hour of the trial arrives.

There is biblical precedence for delayed fulfillment. Satan has been judged, John 12:31, but execution of sentence is yet-future, Revelation 20:10. The Old Testament saints "obtained a good testimony through faith," but they did not receive the promise, Hebrews 11:39. The circumstances that would bring about the fulfillment of the promises did not exist within their lifetime, yet they believed and persevered.

So, too, did the Philadelphians believe and persevere; so has every New Testament believer from that time to this. In delaying the fulfillment of the promise God has provided something better, that the community of faith throughout this church dispensation should receive the promise all at one time. The time for the world-wide trial was future: it will come in relation to the "things which are," Revelation 1:19.

Just as the promise of faith was not only to the patriarchs but also to their (spiritual) heirs, even so the promise to the Philadelphia church is to all who have kept and will keep Jesus' command to persevere. Since it is God who works in us to do his will and good pleasure (Philippians 2:13), then that promise of perseverance and deliverance is for every New Testament believer.

There remains, then, deliverance for the church, i.e., for the church physically alive when the appointed hour arrives. When the hour of trial is about to come upon "those who dwell on the earth," the living church will be delivered ahead of that trial. That is the promise, "I also will keep you out of the hour of the trial."

The post-tribulation view tries to translate *ek* (out of; from) as "during." But the use of the preposition is well-established, and in relation to time it may be translated "from" but never "during." Thus, the majority of translations of 3:10 read "keep you from the hour of the trial." In accordance with the basic meaning of *ek* as "out of," to translate "from" must mean "kept out of" not "kept during." The New Testament church believer is not sustained during the Tribulation period, he or she is kept out of the Tribulation.

Two other views, the midtribulational (sometimes called pre-wrath) and partial rapture views, have the same fault as the posttribulational view: the church endures some or all of the

Tribulation. In the partial rapture view believers are raptured when they become worthy: some before the Tribulation; others during the Tribulation; and still others endure the entire Tribulation (as explained in the first chapter the partial rapture view is heretical).

In the mid-tribulation or "pre-wrath" view the church is raptured when the Antichrist is revealed by his declaration of godhood, 2 Thessalonians 2:3–4; Revelation 13:3–4, on the view that the Tribulation begins when this event occurs. However, the Tribulation begins when Christ breaks the first seal, 6:1, and the Antichrist makes a covenant, Daniel 9:27, and goes out conquering and to conquer, Revelation 6:2. He breaks that covenant midway, Daniel 9:27, an event corresponding to his declaration of godhood.

The word "kept" in Revelation 3:10 is misconstrued by some. It is true, believers are "kept," the Greek *tēréō*, during times of tribulation (*thlípsis*), John 16:33; 17:15; Romans 8:35; 12:12; 2 Corinthians 1:4; 1 Thessalonians 3:4; 1:9; 2:9, 10, 22. The word "tribulation" is generally used in the New Testament to mean a course of persecution and trial. However, "the hour of the trial" in Revelation 3:10 refers to a specific *thlípsis* the Tribulation of Revelation 6–19; Matthew 24:21.

To come to the heart of the matter, the promise of Revelation 3:10 is a promise to deliver the physically living church from the Tribulation period. The members of the New Testament church that are on the earth when the Tribulation is due will be kept "out of" the hour of the trial. The Tribulation is, in the first instance, the time of Israel's trial. As YHWH said so succinctly at Jeremiah 30:7, "That day will be awful, none like it, a time of trouble for Jacob! But he will be delivered out of it." The Old Testament makes very clear that one purpose of the Tribulation event is to restore the nation Israel to its former position of faith in, and as the servant of, YHWH, through faith in Jesus as their Messiah.

Let us consider the timing of the rapture doctrinally. The doctrines of a completed salvation, imputed justification, and positional sanctification compel me to ask, "What would be the purpose of any part of the church—any believer in Christ as Savior—enduring the Tribulation?" A completed salvation means nothing more is required to make the believer worthy of heaven—Jesus paid it all, so I have nothing to do to make me fit for God's presence. Imputed justification means

God sees me in Christ as innocent of the crime of sin—Jesus paid it all, so I am forever free from the penalty of sin. Positional sanctification means God has declared me in Christ to be holy and righteous—Jesus paid it all, so in Christ I am righteous and holy.

Therefore, because every New Testament church dispensation believer from AD 33 to the rapture is saved, justified, and sanctified, what possible reason could God possibly have for making one tiny part of the New Testament church go through the Tribulation? To repeat, *every* New Testament church dispensation believer is saved, justified, righteous, and holy in Christ. If Jesus paid it all—and he did—what might I owe God that would cause me to endure the time of God's wrath against unbelievers, should the Tribulation begin during my lifetime? Nothing, because Jesus paid it all.

The intent of the Tribulation is expressed in Revelation 6:17. It is "The great day of God's wrath; who is able to stand?" The Tribulation is an opportunity for unbelievers to answer that question for faith or no-faith. God's love is always toward his saved people; but his wrath is always toward the unsaved, Psalm 7:11. For those who are saved God's wrath was borne by Christ, so that they will never experience his wrath. There are trials, which are intended to mature the believer, chastisement which is intended recover the sinning believer, but never wrath, which is punishment and strictly penal in nature. The believer's salvation, justification, and sanctification in Christ prevent him or her from suffering God's wrath.

Common sense requires us to bear in mind that, if we are to speak of "the church" during the Tribulation, then we are speaking of a tiny fraction of the total membership of the church, which is every believer from Christ's resurrection to the rapture. Why should one tiny group of New Testament church dispensation believers, out of the whole church from Christ's resurrection into the yet-future, most of whom have died in Christ, why should living believers bear the wrath God intends for unbelievers? Are believers at the close of the church dispensation any less saved, any less justified, any less sanctified than believers at the beginning? No, all are equally saved through faith in the merit of Christ who suffered God's wrath on their behalf.

Some Christians sincerely believe the church alive when the Tribulation begins is not a worthy church, because their faith is weak or lapsed—a Laodicean-type church—and therefore those particular believers must endure sufficient persecution to purge their unworthy faith. Doctrinally, this view says that the payment of Christ for the guilt of sin (his propitiation) was not sufficient for every believer, as though somehow his propitiation will run out of merit at the end of the church dispensation. Logically this view must assume that every living believer in the last days before the Tribulation is a member of the Laodicean church! Perhaps the reader would like to volunteer his or her church as a Laodicean-type church? No? I didn't think so. (And if you do, find another local church.)

The fact is Christ's propitiation is sufficient for every believer throughout the church dispensation: from his resurrection to the rapture of the living church. The facts are that the "church of Laodicea" has existed throughout the church dispensation. The fact is that lapsed or weak faith is to be found throughout the church dispensation.

More to the point, no one is made worthy of heaven by works or trials. Only the merit of Jesus secures heaven for every New Testament believer, including those living in the time just prior to when the Tribulation period will begin. Look at the letter to Laodicea. Jesus did not make an opposite promise to Laodicea, to deliver them "into the hour of the trial." His promise to Laodicea was a genuine offer of fellowship, 3:20. All believers will be "kept out of," not endure through, the Tribulation period.

Those unbelievers who become saved believers during the Tribulation period are not part of the New Testament church. However, they are just as saved. They do not experience God's wrath after salvation, but persecution from the unbelieving world. Many believers do die during the Tribulation, but death is Christ's way of bringing his people to their eternal home cleansed from the presence of sin forever. Many do suffer, but suffering is the portion of God's people while they are in the world.

The effects of God's wrath against unbelievers do fall on his saved people during the Tribulation, just as happens during the church dispensation; just as it has happened for millennia of believers from Adam forward. But those effects are incidental, not penal. God's saved-and-made-righteous-in-Christ people are not suffering God's wrath against the unsaved. When, for example, floods come and bad circumstances happen to everyone in the flood zone, even if the flood was God's wrath against sinners, it was not his wrath against believers, merely the circumstances through which God's wrath against unbelievers was made known.

The point may seem too fine for some, but what is important is God's intent. Righteous suffering under difficult circumstances is God's way to mature the believer in his or her faith, and a God-given opportunity to establish one's testimony when the circumstances are endured in a godly manner. "But if also you should suffer for righteousness, you are blessed" 1 Peter 3:14. God is with the believer to give grace and the blessings of providence to help them bear through the trials formed by the circumstances. Those unsaved at the beginning of the Tribulation who become saved during the Tribulation will suffer difficult circumstances and persecution for righteousness sake, but will not suffer God's wrath because Jesus paid it all.

God is always with the believer to make a way to endure, to give grace to persevere, to mature them in Christ, to deliver them to heaven. All Christians within the New Testament church dispensation suffer the trials and the circumstances of natural and divine events. There is a difference between general trouble (tribulation) and the Tribulation-Day of the Lord period of time. The living church is delivered from the hour of the trial, the Tribulation, because the trial is not meant for the church. That deliverance is the "rapture."

What is the Church?

Reformed theology denies a rapture. Many who claim Reformed theology might be surprised to know that, but only Dispensational theology claims a rapture. Many non-Dispensationalists who claim a rapture might also be surprised to learn only Dispensational theology claims a rapture. It all comes down to eschatology, the doctrine of last things, specifically that aspect of eschatology either favoring or denying the Davidic-Messianic Kingdom will be conducted by Christ, on this present earth, between the second advent and the Great White Throne judgment, enduring to a thousand years (a millennium).

Reformed views on a Davidic-Messianic-Millennial Kingdom after the second advent divide into one of two positions.

> Amillennialism. Literally "no-millennium." The eschatological doctrine that the world will become more and more unrighteous until Christ returns to resurrect the dead and then judge the living and dead to determine their eternity in heaven or in hell [Boettner, 4], and then the kingdom, Revelation 21–22.

> Postmillennialism. Literally "after the millennium." The eschatological theology that the church and the Holy Spirit will, through the gospel, make the world a place of peace and righteousness, a condition which will last for an undetermined period of time. At the end of that time Christ will return to receive the kingdom created by the church and Holy Spirit, followed by a general resurrection, and then judgment of living and dead as to eternity in heaven or hell [Boettner, 4] and then the eternal state, Revelation 21–22.

The Dispensational view is known as premillennialism: Christ's second advent ushers in a literal, earthly Davidic-Messianic-Millennial Kingdom.

You ask, "What does Reformed eschatology have to do with the New Testament church and the rapture?" The answer is not complicated, but has a few moving parts.

The kingdom—the Davidic-Messianic Kingdom—is that kingdom promised to national ethnic Israel, through King David, at 2 Samuel 7:13, 16, and further explained by David at Psalm 2, to be fulfilled in the Christ, Psalm 2:2.

One of the purposes of the Tribulation is to prepare national ethnic Israel for that coming kingdom. But Reformed theology says God abandoned national ethnic Israel to make the New Testament church a new Israel, or continuation of Israel (depending on which Reformed theologian one asks), and therefore that promised Davidic-Messianic Kingdom is to be fulfilled by the New Testament church in this present world (postmillennialism), or in the new heavens and earth to come (Amillennialism). Or in heaven during this present time according to some Reformed.

So if the New Testament church is the promised Davidic Kingdom of the Messiah, or if the New Testament church is creating the promised Davidic Kingdom of the Messiah, then there is no need of a tribulation or a rapture, because the New Testament church is really a new Israel that spiritually fulfills some of God's promises to national ethnic Old Testament Israel (but not all, for some will not be fulfilled).

Therefore, whether the New Testament church is really a new Israel, or not, matters to the doctrines of the rapture and the tribulation. The question to be answered is this, what is the church?

The first Reformers, and currently Reformed theology, defined the church as that body of believers from Adam to the last person saved prior to return of Christ and final judgment. This doctrine ignores the simple fact God has and will have many people groups of those he saved.

Saved pre-Noahic Flood.

Saved post-Noahic Flood.

Saved physical descendants of Abraham.

Saved under the Mosaic Law.

Saved between Christ's resurrection and the rapture.

Saved during the Tribulation.

Saved during the Davidic-Messianic Kingdom.

The New Testament church is one of those people groups, saved in the same way others were saved: faith in God and God's historically current testimony, as given in the progressive revelation of truth, as to the way of salvation.

Reformed theology also redefines national ethnic Israel as the New

Testament church. One prominent amillennial theologian has captured the basic belief of non-dispensationalists concerning the relation of church and Israel. He wrote,

> To say the church supplants, replaces, or displaces Israel does not accurately represent my view as an Amillennialist . . . I certainly think that the church as the New Israel surpasses the Old Israel . . . The butterfly does not exactly replace the caterpillar. *It is the caterpillar in a new phase of existence*. In the same way, to speak of the Church replacing Israel is to forget that the Church *is* Israel in a newly reformed and expanded phase of existence . . . the Church is really the continuation of Israel [Waldron, 6–7, emphasis original].

Does the Scripture support that interpretation?

What is the Church?

In Dispensational theology, the church is a body of New Testament believers called out from the world by Christ to worship and serve and have fellowship with God Father-Son-Spirit. The New Testament church consists of those saved persons between Christ's resurrection and his gathering the New Testament church to himself at the rapture.

Some of the distinctives of the New Testament church are indwelt by the Holy Spirit, no tent or building or place necessary for worship (each believer is a temple of God, 1 Corinthians 6:19; 2 Corinthians 6:16, and therefore he or she may worship God in spirit and truth at any time in any place).

The New Testament church, corporately and as individual believers, is the body of Christ, 1 Corinthians 12:27, a holy temple to the Lord, Ephesians 2:21, and always present with the Lord, even as Christ prayed to the Father, John 17:24, "Father, those you have given me, I desire that where I am they also might be with me, that they might behold my glory that you gave me because you loved me before the foundation of the world."

Is the New Testament Church the New Israel? The following section discusses that doctrine in depth.

Overview

The reader should know I accurately label myself as Dispensational and Reformed. My personal doctrinal statement contains

Dispensational and Reformed elements. Dispensationalism is primarily concerned with the doctrines ecclesiology (church) and eschatology (end times). What is Dispensational theology?

> Theology is the science that seeks to understand God and his interactions with his creation through systematic study of God's revelation of himself in the Bible.

> Dispensationalism is a systematic method of understanding history as a series of God-initiated economies, or "dispensations," by consistently applying the principles of the Literal (grammatical-historical) hermeneutic to all scriptures.

> Dispensational theology is that branch of the science of theology that seeks to understand God and his interactions with his creation, as God has revealed himself in the Bible through a series of God-initiated economies, or "dispensations," by consistently applying the principles of the Literal (grammatical-historical) hermeneutic to all scriptures.

A Dispensationalist consistently applies to all Scripture a method of interpretation known as the Literal hermeneutic, which seeks the normal or plain understanding of language. The Literal hermeneutic is also known as the grammatical-historical hermeneutic.

Dispensationalism maintains a distinction between national ethnic Israel and the New Testament Church, in the past, in the present, and into the future. Dispensationalism understands the New Testament church has neither replaced, nor superseded, nor is the natural evolution of national ethnic Israel in the future plans of God. Both Israel and the New Testament church exist side-by-side in the yet-future plans of God, with different but compatible destinies.

(For a brief study of Dispensationalism see my book *A Primer on Dispensationalism*. For an in depth study see the *Primer's* big brother, *Understanding Dispensational Theology*.)

One of the essential characteristics of dispensational theology is that "a dispensationalist keeps Israel and the church distinct." A dispensationalist believes the literal hermeneutic reveals God has a program for Israel and a separate program for the church.

In my understanding these two programs overlap at certain points, but otherwise are separate, requiring specific plans and processes for the fulfillment of each. God has a program for other groups as well, e.g., the holy angels, the fallen angels, unsaved human beings, the non-Jewish nations, those persons saved from Adam to Abraham, those descended from Abraham, the Tribulation martyrs, and the millennial saints. God has a distinct program for national ethnic Israel and a distinct program for the New Testament church.

The Dispensationalist's interpretive conclusion differs from Reformed and other theologies. These theologies do not interpret Old Testament eschatological prophecies using the literal methodology. They believe in an allegorical and spiritualizing method of interpretation which views Old Testament prophecies made to Israel as really made for the New Testament church. Put more clearly, non-dispensational theologies believe promises which seemed at the time to have been intended for national ethnic Israel were actually intended for a new yet-future Israel, which is defined by these non-dispensational theologies as the New Testament church.

Because of their interpretive methodology, non-dispensationalists do not find a millennium in Old or New Testament prophecy, nor the salvation of national ethnic Israel at the second advent. There are variations to the non-dispensationalist position in which there is some kind of kingdom, literal or non-literal, and there is salvation for individual members of national ethnic Israel, but not a national salvation. And there are variations where there is no millennium kingdom and there is no salvation for national ethnic Israel. In every non-literal interpretation of Old and New Testament eschatology by any theological system other than Dispensationalism, there is no independent future for national ethnic Israel.

The Dispensationalist believes Christ will save national ethnic Israel at the beginning of his Davidic-Messianic-Millennial kingdom. Romans 11:26 is one supporting Scripture: "and so all Israel will be saved." After making that prophecy Paul quotes Isaiah 59:20, 21, to support the salvation of national ethnic Israel at the second advent. The Dispensationalist bases the restoration of national ethnic Israel on many Old Testament and New Testament verses.

Perhaps one clear New Testament verse is enough to dispel the notion the New Testament church is really a new Israel in the purpose, plans, and processes of God.

>1 Corinthians 10:32, And you do not give offense to Jewish and Greeks and to the church of God.

The Holy Spirit consistently divides the world's people into three distinct groups: Jews, non-Jews ("Greeks"), and the "church of God" which is composed of all former Jews and non-Jews who have become Christians. "Jews" are not just Israelis but also those gentiles who convert to Judaism, the religion of the Jews. "Greeks" are not only Grecians but are every nationality or ethnicity that isn't national ethnic Israel.

This view can be taken of "Jew" and "Greek" because the "church of God" is every Hebrew or gentile who has been or will be saved between Christ's resurrection and the rapture. The "church of God" then, is neither Hebrew/Jew/Judaism nor Greek/gentile/pagan, but a separate group of people saved out of those other people groups: the "church of God" is the New Testament church. Just as the New Testament church is not a continuation of Greek/gentile/pagan peoples, so it is not a continuation of Hebrew/Jew/Judaism peoples.

The Greek text of 1 Corinthians 10:32 does not have the definite article before "Jews" or "Greeks" as it does before "church." When the definite article is present it specifies a certain person, place, or thing. When the article is absent the quality or character of a person, place, or thing is emphasized. Paul wanted to specifically identify that particular people group known as *the* church. He wanted to emphasize some quality belonging to the terms "Jew" and "Greek."

The verse may be interpretively paraphrased in a way to reflect the grammar: "give no offense to Israel, gentiles, or the New Testament church of God in Christ." Paul and the Holy Spirit make a distinction between national ethnic Israel and the church. Paul does not believe and the Holy Spirit does not teach that the New Testament church has surpassed national ethnic Israel as some sort of New Israel. They make a clear distinction between the "church of God" and the people group Hebrew/Jew/Judaism.

In terms of this discussion, what the Non-dispensational view means is that unfulfilled prophecies concerning national ethnic Israel will not be fulfilled by or for national ethnic Israel, but will be fulfilled non-literally by or for the New Testament church.

Put another way, in the Non-dispensational view there is no more national ethnic Israel in God's purpose, but a new non-literal, spiritualized "Israel" which is the New Testament church. In the Non-dispensational view the fulfillment of some prophecies cannot be literal. For example, literal possession of the physical land Palestine must be eliminated from prophecy, or fulfilled in a non-literal fashion that spiritualizes the land. Both the rapture and Tribulation are unnecessary and will not literally take place. The Non-dispensationalists' rejection of national ethnic Israel and their allegorical or spiritualized interpretation of eschatological prophecy related to national ethnic Israel requires a non-literal hermeneutic, and so is rejected by the Dispensationalist.

Dispensational theology believes as-yet-unfulfilled prophecies made to national ethnic Israel will be fulfilled in the future by or for national ethnic Israel. That means prophecies specifically related to the New Testament church, such as the rapture, will also be literally fulfilled. In the next section I will address why Dispensational theology believes national ethnic Israel continues to retain its prophetic future. And if Israel, so also the New Testament church, the rapture, and the Tribulation.

The Word/Name/Nation/People Israel

The New Testament authors were very clear that the church is not some sort of New Israel or spiritualized Israel. When the literal hermeneutic is consistently applied to New Testament texts, one discovers the term "Israel" always refers to national ethnic Israel. See Fruchtenbaum [684] for a list with brief analysis of each verse. (Or like the Bereans, Acts 17:11, search the scriptures using a concordance for your Bible version.)

There is no comingling or confusion of the distinctive terms "Israel" and "church" in the New Testament texts. A simple matter of definition demonstrates the differences between Israel and the New Testament church. Scripture doesn't define, it describes, but from observation and description one is able to develop a definition. The interpretive method one uses is critical to defining the terms. Under a literal hermeneutic "Israel" in the Old Testament is [Harrison, s. v. Israel]:

The name God gave Jacob, Genesis 32:28.

The name given the descendants of Jacob-Israel's twelve sons who collectively form the nation of Israel, Exodus 3:16.

The kingdom developed under Saul, David, and Solomon comprised of the united twelve tribes of Israel, 1 Samuel 8—1 Kings 11.

The name of the northern kingdom formed by Rehoboam after Solomon's death, 1 Kings 12:25–14:20.

The name for the nation rebuilt by the returned Babylonian exiles until AD 70, resumed May 14, 1948.

The collective name given common persons in the nation as distinguished from the priests, Levites, and other ministers, Ezra 6:16; 9:1; 10:25; Nehemiah 11:3, etc.

A spiritual designation given to Messiah as the representative and king of the nation, Hosea 11:1 with Matthew 2:15.

Israel in the New Testament is:

A name given to saved Israelis as the true Israel of God, Galatians 6:16 (discussed below).

The people and the land of those people, e.g., Matthew 2:6, 20.

All Israelis, e.g., Matthew 2:6; a select group of Israelis, e.g., Luke 4:25, 27; Israelis who have been born-again, e.g., Galatians 6:16; saved and unsaved Israelis, e.g., Romans 9:6.

National ethnic Israel. From Abraham forward, e.g., Luke 2:25; at a particular time in history, e.g., Acts 13:17; currently-living, e.g., Matthew 8:10.

Unbelieving Israelis, e.g., Acts 3:12.

Those who want to believe the word Israel sometimes means the New Testament church point to Romans 9:6; 11:26; and Galatians 6:16. I will examine those three and a few other uses that might be questioned.

Selected Uses Of The Term "Israel" Explained

Acts 28:20. Paul refers to the "Hope of Israel." Paul is speaking to Jews, v. 17. The Hope of Israel was a term used by the Jews for their Messianic expectations. This does not deny the Christ was also the hope of the gentiles. However, the "Hope of Israel" was a cultural term specific to national ethnic Israel, not the New Testament church.

Romans 9:6. The context is set by the reference to national ethnic Israel in v. 3. Paul thought of himself as a Jew, therefore his "countrymen according to the flesh" were Jews. The sum of Paul's argument in this section is that the circumstances of natural birth do not make a person part of the community of the saved (cf. John 1:12–13). The unsaved Israeli is identified here as "they are not all Israel who are of Israel." One is an Israeli by natural birth, but belongs to God only by the new birth, whether that new birth occurred during the Old or New Testament times. Paul is not here speaking of gentiles, whom he doesn't introduce into his argument until 9:24. The section, 9:1–23, is all about saved Israelis in national ethnic Israel. Only those Israelis who have faith like Abraham's faith are saved. Compare the use of "O man" in 9:20 with the definition of the term established in 2:2, where it can only mean national ethnic Israel, and compare 2:17.

Romans 9:27. Paul quoting Isaiah speaking to Israel can only mean national ethnic Israel is in view in the Romans' text (unless a baseless assumption is made that Israel means the New Testament church). Paul begins with Hosea in 9:25, speaking of the gentiles responding to God's call, then says most of national ethnic Israel will not listen to God's call, a fact confirmed by the remainder of the argument. By the way, the argument here is eschatological, see 9:28. In the future a remnant of national ethnic Israel will be saved. Saved for what? The original reference to "sand of the sea," was in the context of Abraham's descendants inheriting the land, "your descendants will possess the gates of their enemies," Genesis 22:17, "I will give to your descendants all these lands," Genesis 26:4. Abraham's descendants are physical, the "sand," and by faith, the "stars." The eschatological remnant of "sand" in the context of Romans 9:27–28 must be national ethnic Israel. Saved Israelis of national ethnic Israel will inherit the land, a literal physical possession for a literal national ethnic Israel.

Romans 9:31. Those in national ethnic Israel who pursued righteousness (salvation) through obedience to the Mosaic law, v. 32, did not achieve the salvation they hoped for. In 9:33 Paul makes clear their salvation lay in accepting Christ. National ethnic Israel did not find salvation through the legal works of the Mosaic Law, but can find salvation through faith in Christ in this New Testament church dispensation. Since members of national ethnic Israel are able through salvation to become members of the New Testament church, then the New Testament church and national ethnic Israel must be two separate people groups in the New Testament church dispensation. The New Testament church cannot be some sort of Israel in a newly reformed and expanded phase of existence since 1) national ethnic Israel still exists as part of the purpose, plans, and processes of God; 2) Israelis are saved out of national ethnic Israel into the New Testament church; 3) a remnant of national ethnic Israel will be saved in the future—future to the New Testament church dispensation.

Romans 10:19. Paul is using Isaiah at Romans 10:15, 16 to speak of national ethnic Israel in Paul's day at Romans 10:19. Moreover, in 10:19 national ethnic Israel is contrasted with the gentiles, "those who are not a nation." National ethnic Israel continues to be part of the purpose, plans, and processes of God.

Romans 10:21. The identity of "but to Israel he says" is established as national ethnic Israel by what has gone before. God's hands remain outstretched to national ethnic Israel in the offer of salvation. In the dispensation of the New Testament church salvation will make individual Israelis Christians and members of the church. After the second advent, "when all Israel will be saved," 11:26 (see below) Christ will save national ethnic Israel.

Romans 11:7. The identity of "Israel" in 11:7 is set at 11:1 as national ethnic Israel. The mention in 11:4 of the 7,000 reserved to God in Elijah's day indicates that during the New Testament church dispensation some out of national ethnic Israel will be saved, others will not. However, lack of salvation for some does not eliminate the nation Israel in God's eschatological purpose, plans, and processes.

Romans 11:26. The preceding context, which began at 11:1, and the reference to "Jacob," indicates the people group in view is national ethnic Israel. "Jacob" is an Old Testament term identifying God's people group national ethnic Israel. For example, 1 Samuel 12:8; 2 Samuel 23:1; 1 Chronicles 16:13; Psalm 14:7; Psalm 114:7; Psalm 135:4; Isaiah 60:16; 65:9; Jeremiah 46:27–28; Ezekiel 39:25. The texts in Isaiah, Jeremiah, and Ezekiel are eschatological prophecies.

The context of Romans 11:26 is eschatological. Paul uses the future tense: then all Israel "will be" saved, a verb in the future indicative passive, third person singular. Paul knows Messiah has come once, the first advent. Paul has previously said that members of national ethnic Israel are being saved to become members of the New Testament church as a result of that first advent. Paul's use of Isaiah 59:20–21; 27:9 must be a reference to the second advent. When Messiah comes the second time then-living members of national ethnic Israel will be saved. God has a purpose for national ethnic Israel.

Galatians 6:16. Discussed below.

Ephesians 2:12. Since the contrast is between gentiles as a people group and the "commonwealth" of Israel as a people group, then "Israel" must refer to national ethnic Israel.

Further Discussion In Romans

The context of Romans 2 is the members of national ethnic Israel, see v. 12, 17, 25, 29. Romans 2:29–30 might be misunderstood to mean the New Testament church, but the reference to the distinctly Jewish practice of circumcision makes that identification impossible. In Romans 2 Paul sets the contextual stage for later arguments, where the true Israeli is the one who has believed in Jesus the Savior.

Romans 9–11 presents a constant contrast between unbelieving Israelis who are not saved and believing Israelis who are saved. The end of the contrast is a prophecy that all national ethnic Israel will be saved at a future date, 11:26–27. In Romans 9, the definition of those who are "not Israel" are those in national ethnic Israel who during the New Testament church dispensation have not believed in Jesus the Savior. Those who are "Israel" are those in national ethnic Israel who during the New Testament church dispensation have believed in Jesus the Savior. When Messiah returns the church will return with him (Revelation 19:14, "armies of heaven") and national ethnic Israel alive at his return will be saved, Zechariah 9:16; 10:6–12; 12:7; 13:1; 14:11.

Looking into the revealed future, there will be a judgment of re-gathered Jews who survived the Tribulation, Ezekiel 20:33–44. Some surviving Jews will be saved, but others will not. Which Jews will not be saved? Further revelation provides the answer: those who received the mark of the (Antichrist-) beast will not be saved, Revelation 14:9–11. Those who did not receive the mark will be saved, Isaiah 66:7–8 and the aforementioned passages in Zechariah.

Paul did not know about the mark of the beast, but Paul knew that some Jews would not be saved when Christ returned, because Paul knew that salvation is a matter of faith. Why then does Paul say "all" Israel will be saved when Christ returns? This statement may be understood by reference to the salvation of Jews currently occurring during the New Testament church dispensation. Not all Jews will be saved during this dispensation, yet Paul says God has not cast away his people Israel, 11:1. So even though there will be unsaved Jews during the church dispensation, God has not cast away his people, for some are saved.

In like manner, even though not all Jews will be saved when Christ returns (Ezekiel 20:38, Revelation 14:9–11), yet God has not cast away his people Israel. So in Paul's future view at Romans 11:26, "all" must be understood in the context of the completed revelation. "All" excludes those who will have placed themselves under judgment by worshiping the Antichrist-beast. Or as Isaiah said, 59:20, the Redeemer will come to Zion and to those in Jacob who turn from transgression.

Those Israelis who are saved in the current New Testament church dispensation are part of the New Testament church composed of converted Jews and converted pagans. The two groups have been merged by the Spirit to form the church, Ephesians 2:11–22. The church is a new people group neither Jew nor pagan, neither Hebrew nor gentile, but a new people group in Christ. Therefore the New Testament church cannot be a newly reformed and expanded phase of Israel, cannot be the continuation of Israel, and cannot be Israel. To return to Waldron's caterpillar-butterfly metaphor, the caterpillar is not Israel but the promises made to Abraham, which over time became Jacob-Israel the butterfly. The butterfly national ethnic Israel has an eschatological future independent of the New Testament church.

Discussion Of Faith In Galatians

This section is preparation for the discussion of Galatians 6:16. The "sons of Abraham," Galatians 3:7, are those who have the same quality of faith as Abraham—not the same content of faith, but the same steadfast confidence in the promises God made to them. As Ryrie has said.

The basis of salvation in every age is the death of Christ; the requirement for salvation in every age is faith; the object of faith in every age is God; the content of faith changes in the various dispensations [Charles Ryrie, *Dispensationalism*, 115].

"Content of faith" is a term that describes God's testimony in history as the means by which God's grace in salvation is accessed. The sinner is always saved by God's grace through the sinner's faith in God, through God's historically current testimony as given in the progressive revelation of truth.

The doctrine of progressive revelation is the simple observation God does not reveal all things at the same time, but over time God's revelation is completed. As God said through Isaiah 28:10 (ESV), "For it is precept upon precept, precept upon precept, line upon line, line upon line, here a little, there a little."

The content of faith changes as God progressively gives new revelation and changes the economies (dispensations) through which he administers his affairs in the world. As faith is the means by which God's grace in salvation is accessed, the content of faith (God's testimony), was the historical means whereby God's grace was accessed in the various dispensations.

Every sinner, from Adam forward, who has had faith in God's way of salvation, as revealed by the content of faith they received from God, is saved, sealed, and secured in his or her faith by the Spirit. If, as is the case, the one and only basis of salvation is the propitiation for sin made by Christ, then it is the merit of Christ applied by the Spirit that saves the soul and secures the believer in his or her salvation. The divine means of salvation has not changed from Adam forward: the Spirit applies the merits of Christ by grace through the sinner's faith to meet the sinner's spiritual need and effect and secure salvation. If salvation is the same in both Testaments—not the content of faith or the means of grace, but the rescue of the soul from the penalty of sin by the merit of Christ—then the way salvation was and is secured must be the same: by grace through faith.

Old and New Testament believers are "sons of Abraham" in the sense their faith was the same quality as Abraham's faith. More simply, Abraham is the scriptural example of saved by grace through faith, an example that describes every saved person's salvation experience.

In the Bible the term "sons of," when not used of a physical relationship, indicates one has a quality or characteristic of the person or thing he or she is a "son of." The "sons of light," 1 Thessalonians 5:5, have salvation and understanding. The "sons of disobedience," Ephesians 5:6; Colossians 3:6, are unredeemed sinners whose immoral character and actions are described in Ephesians 5:3–5; Colossians 3:5. The sons of God are those who are in a faith-based relation with God, possessing his righteousness (by imputation) and living righteously. The sons of Abraham are those who possess the same quality and character of faith as Abraham.

Abraham believed in the promise that through his seed—through one begotten from him—"all the families of the earth would be blessed." Historically that seed was Isaac, through whom the promised blessing flowed to future generations, until that one seed was born in whom the promise would be completely fulfilled. Paul identifies that one singular seed as Christ, Galatians 3:16. The promised blessing originated because of Abraham's faith—for the Christ came through his loins because of his faith—therefore all who are saved by like faith (the quality of faith that trusts in God's promises) are "sons of" Abraham.

Paul's argument in Galatians has nothing to do with the church receiving the promises concerning national ethnic Israel made to Abraham, less still that the church is some sort of New Israel. One must keep the context in mind. Paul's argument to the Galatians can be summarized as "do not return to the Law of Moses" (see Acts 15:1). The promise of salvation by faith made to Abraham was before the Mosaic Law and the Law did not abrogate the promise. Therefore, those who have received the promise cannot be made perfect by the Law. That is the context and that is the sum of the argument. The Law remains what it always was: an accuser of sin and a moral guide to righteousness.

"Those who are of faith are sons of Abraham." This direct statement includes everyone who was saved by faith, whether an Israeli or a gentile; whether Old Testament or New Testament. This statement does not mean a believer in one dispensation has become through salvation a "newly reformed and expanded phase" (Waldron) of another group of believers in a prior dispensation. Who would be so foolish to say Abraham was Noah in a newly reformed and expanded phase of existence; that Abraham was really the continuation of Noah? Or that Noah was really the continuation of Seth, or Enoch, or even his father Lamech? Yet there are those who foolishly say the New Testament church has become some sort of New Israel which has surpassed the Old Israel—that the church is Israel, a continuation of the Old Israel. Scripture settles the matter: the sinner saved in the New Testament church dispensation is called a "son of Abraham" because of his or her faith, but is *never* called a son of Moses, or a son of the Law, or a son of Israel.

Galatians 6:16

Galatians 6:16 is the only New Testament verse where "Israel" might mean the New Testament church. "And as many who by this rule will conduct their manner of life, peace upon them, and mercy; and mercy upon the Israel of God."

There are two possible interpretations of "Israel" based on the Greek *kai* ("and") in the phrase "and upon the Israel" etc. The *kai* could be copulative (joining, connecting) or epexegetical (explicative, explaining). Neither a copulative nor an epexegetical *kai* supports this phrase as referring to any Israeli other than Israelis who were by birth members of national ethnic Israel and had become Christians through salvation by faith in Jesus.

If the *kai* is copulative, then Paul is referring to two groups of people. Paul says salvation makes a new person. He mentions two groups of saved people in 6:12, 13, 15. The two groups were those saved persons in the Galatian church who were circumcised and those saved persons in the Galatian church who were uncircumcised. This is the same Israeli-gentile division as at 2:7–9. There, the circumcised believers wanted the uncircumcised believers to become circumcised. All in both groups are believers. What does Paul say about these two groups of believers?

"In 6:16, Paul pronounces a blessing on members of the two groups who would follow the rule of salvation through faith alone. The first group is the 'them,' the uncircumcision . . . the second group is the 'Israel of God.' These are the circumcision, the Jewish believers who, in contrast with the Judaizers, followed the rule of salvation by grace through faith alone" [Fruchtenbaum, 691]. The circumcised believers had been persuaded that their circumcision made them a better class of believers because they were following Christ *and* the Law. If it made them better believers, then it would surely do the same for their uncircumcised fellow believers. Paul's letter was written to refute that notion.

Paul begins v. 16, "and as many as walk according to this rule." Eadie says, "the 'many' may not be gentile believers as such and opposed [contrasted] to Jewish believers, but [may be] the entire number who walk according to this rule; while Paul finds among them a certain class to whom his heart turns with instinctive fondness—'the Israel of God' . . . To the apostle there were two Israels—'they are not all Israel which are of Israel,'—and he says here, not Israel according to the flesh, but 'the Israel of God,' or the true believing Israel; his own brethren by a double tie—by blood, and especially by grace" [Eadie, 1:471].

More simply, Eadie is saying that in the one church Paul recognized two groups of believers: those who were gentile by natural birth and those who were Israeli by natural birth; but all were saved by the new birth and together formed the church in Galatia. He fondly addressed the Israeli believers as the Israel of God, because they were his brethren by physical lineage and by saving faith in Christ. These lived according to the rule of saved by grace alone through faith alone in Jesus the only way and only means of salvation.

The *kai* could be epexegetical, which is the NIV translation, "Peace and mercy to all who follow this rule, even to the Israel of God." Hogg and Vine [341–342] believed the *kai* was epexegetical, and stated, "the ideal to which the title pointed had been realized only by the few among their successive generations . . . the true Israelite is he who, of whatever nation born, puts his faith in God." Hogg and Vine inserted an explanation to make sure they were not misunderstood, "It is not, however, to this Israel after the Spirit that the distinctive promises of national restoration and blessing, see Romans 11:26, 27, will be fulfilled, but to 'Israel after the flesh,' 1 Corinthians 10:18, the natural descendants of Abraham through Jacob."

Burton says [357–358], "There is, in fact, no instance of Paul using 'Israel' except of the Jewish nation or a part thereof . . . in view of the phrase 'of God' the expression applies not to the whole Jewish nation, but to the pious Israel, the remnant according to the election of grace." On this ground Burton rearranges the verse: "And as many as shall walk by this rule, peace be upon them, and mercy upon the Israel of God." Thus, Burton also identifies the "Israel of God," with the "circumcision" of v. 15 who had believed and were saved by grace through faith.

Longnecker [296–299] believes the *kai* is epexegetical. He notes that "the term 'Israel' is never applied elsewhere in the New Testament to gentile Christians but always to Jews." He then interprets "Israel of God," as follows: "it seems better to argue that here Paul is using a self-designation of his Jewish-Christian opponents in Galatia . . . who used this phrase to assure Paul's gentile converts that by observing the God-given Jewish laws they would become fully 'the Israel of God.' If that be the case, Paul climaxes his response to the Judaizing threat by saying that what the Judaizers were claiming to offer his converts they already have in Christ by faith . . . so properly [they] can be called the Israel of God together with all Jews who believe."

Another view of this passage is given by Ryrie [*Premillennial Faith*, 68–69], who understands the *kai* as copulative, quoting Ellicott, the biblical Greek scholar. "Still, as it is doubtful whether *kai* is ever used by St. Paul in so *marked* an explicative [epexegetical] force as must be assigned . . . and as it seems still more doubtful whether Christians generally could be called the *'Israel* of God' . . . the simple copulative meaning seems more probable."

Ryrie gives his own opinion: "The apostle is singling out believing Jews in this benediction pronounced upon the entire body of Christ, which, of course, includes these Jews . . . It is another indication that gentile and Jewish believers are on the same level since the conjunction links coordinate parts of the sentence. The apostle is invoking blessing upon all who walk according to the rule of grace; then, lest there be any misunderstanding regarding his attitude, he singles out believing Israelites as a special group."

The *kai* is most likely copulative, but whether the copulative or epexegetical, these commentators and Greek scholars agree that at Galatians 6:16 the word "Israel" does not mean the New Testament church is a New Israel surpassing the Old Israel. There is no "Old" or "New" Israel, just national ethnic Israel.

To summarize this section, in every instance where the word "Israel" is found in the New Testament, if one does not allegorize the passage, "Israel" means national ethnic Israel.

Discussion Of The New Testament Church

The Word/Name/People Church

What does the word "church" mean in the New Testament? The word church is the translation of the Greek *ekklēsía* (sometimes spelled *ecclēsía*) [Zodhiates, s. v. 1577], which means a called out assembly. When *ekklēsía* is used of an assembly of saved people in the New Testament dispensation, with few exceptions it designates the New Testament church, the body of Christ as indwelt by the Holy Spirit, and usually means what we think of as a local New Testament church.

The word *ekklēsía* occurs one hundred fourteen times in the New Testament. In Acts 19:32, 39, 41 it refers to an illegal assembly of the citizens of Ephesus. In Hebrews 2:12 and 12:23 it should be translated "assembly." In the following verses it refers to the church as a whole, that is, local churches collectively viewed as one body of Christ: Acts 20:28; 1 Corinthians 10:32; 12:28; Galatians 1:13; Ephesians 1:22; 3:10, 21; 5:23–25, 27, 29, 32; Philippians 3:6; Colossians 1:18, 24. In every other use it means a local New Testament church.

Thus, *ekklēsía* refers to the New Testament church one hundred nine times, and to a local New Testament church ninety-three of those one hundred nine times. Five times *ekklēsía* means an assembly, but two of those times *ekklēsía* refers to an assembly of believers in Jesus the Savior. So, in only three uses, Acts 19:32, 39, 41, does *ekklēsía* not refer to the New Testament church, a body of New Testament believers in Jesus the Savior. The word *ekklēsía* is never used to mean the New Testament church is some sort of New Israel, or continuation of Israel, or is Israel, whether literally, symbolically, spiritually, or allegorically.

Two times *ekklēsía* refers to an assembly of believers. Hebrews 2:12 is a quote from Psalm 22:22, which in its original context referred to believers in YHWH in national ethnic Israel, but in its use in Hebrews' refers to all believers from Adam forward, which is why it should be translated "assembly." Hebrews 12:23 also refers to all the saved from every dispensation, which is why it should be translated "assembly." When every use is carefully considered one discovers that the word *ekklēsía* never means national ethnic Israel, although in Hebrews 2:12 and 12:23 it includes believers who by birth are national ethnic Israelis. Only by allegorizing *ekklēsía* can the New Testament church become some sort of "New Israel."

The New Testament Church Is A New People Group

The New Testament church was not revealed in the Old Testament scriptures. The church was revealed in the New Testament as a necessary and dynamic part of the plans and processes of God, as a program separate from national ethnic Israel. The church was not "new" in relation to God's purpose, plans, and processes, because these were foreordained before the act of creation. The church was "new" in relation to revealed knowledge, i.e., the understanding the Old Testament peoples had achieved about Scripture. Because the Holy Spirit is the one who gives understanding, we can say that the understanding of the New Testament church dispensation was withheld by God from the Old Testament peoples.

The mystery of the church dispensation is that within the New Testament church there are no more Jew and gentile in the religious and spiritual sense. That was Paul's argument in Ephesians 2:14 ff.

> Christ has broken down the religious fence separating Jew and gentile, by abolishing the enmity created by the commandments contained in the Mosaic regulations. He did this by suffering the penalty of the Law, on the cross, thereby effecting reconciliation to God (for those who believe). Thus, in reconciling Jew and gentile to God through the cross, he has eliminated the causes that kept these two peoples separated from one another. In that reconciliation Christ has joined Jew and gentile together in one faith community. In spiritual terms he has made them one body in himself. In making them one body, he has created a new thing which is neither Jew nor gentile, but is a "new man," the body of believers in Christ Jesus. [Quiggle, *Ephesians*, 147.]

Using the literal hermeneutic, several definitions may be developed for the New Testament church by observing Scripture. The New Testament church is:

> All born-again persons living between Christ's resurrection and the rapture, inclusive. These saved persons collectively

comprise the body of Christ indwelt by the Holy Spirit.

A spiritual organism composed of living saved individuals joined together by the operation of the indwelling Holy Spirit so that each can make vital contributions to the work and welfare of the faith community in Christ.

An organization composed of living saved individuals committed to working together to manage a local church's material resources and present a collective witness of faith, doctrine, and practice.

A local body of saved baptized believers, joined together upon a credible profession of saved by grace through faith in Christ the only Savior, regularly meeting together under the leadership of elders and deacons, participating together in a common purpose to worship God, to propagate the Gospel locally and worldwide, to make disciples, to observe the ordinances of baptism and the Lord's supper, to present a common witness of faith and doctrine centered on the word of God, and to encourage one another in the daily practice of the principles, precepts, and values of God as expressed in his Word.

The New Testament church is not an outgrowth or continuation of Judaism, still less a New Israel surpassing the Old Israel. Let us be bluntly honest with the non-dispensational view stated at the beginning of the chapter, which I will repeat here:

I certainly think that the church as the New Israel surpasses the Old Israel . . . The butterfly does not exactly replace the caterpillar. *It is the caterpillar in a new phase of existence*. In the same way, to speak of the Church replacing Israel is to forget that the Church *is* Israel in a newly reformed and expanded phase of existence . . . the Church is really the continuation of Israel. [Waldron, 6–7 (emphasis original).]

If the New Testament church "surpasses Israel," if the New Testament church "*is* Israel," if the New Testament church "is really the continuation of Israel," then the non-dispensational view is that the New Testament church has replaced national ethnic Israel in the purpose, plans, and processes of God.

The non-dispensational view means nothing less than God abandoned his covenant people national ethnic Israel and his covenant promises to those people. That ugly truth of the non-dispensational view is why the non-dispensationalist uses words such as "surpasses," rather than the more truthful word "replaces." The non-dispensational view means God cannot be trusted to keep his word, for the covenant he had with national ethnic Israel began with an unconditional covenant with Abraham, the father of Isaac and Jacob-Israel who inherited the promises—a covenant that is clearly unconditional because only God "signed" the contract, Genesis 12:1–3; 15:4–18; 17:4–8.

The non-dispensationalist will cry, "No, no, God did not break his promises, he is keeping his promises to the Old Israel through the New Israel." But that is foolish. The promises were made to a literal people group.

When God gave promises to the people of national ethnic Israel did he cross his fingers behind his back because he really meant those promises to be the inheritance of the New Testament church? Certainly the Old Testament saints *did not* understand the covenant promises in that manner. On the basis of faith in the covenant promises the Old Testament saints were tortured, stoned, chained, imprisoned, mocked, scourged, sawn in two, tempted, and slain, because they believed the promises were for them and their physical heirs. Let God be true but every man a liar, Romans 3:4, the promises were meant for the people group to whom they were given.

If the New Testament church is the New Israel, then some promises made to the "Old Israel" must be eliminated because they cannot be kept by the New Testament church; others must be fulfilled symbolically because they cannot be fulfilled literally. The undeniable fact is that God made unconditional covenants—Abrahamic, Land, Davidic, and New—with national ethnic Israel, not with some spiritual "continuation." Who can trust a God who breaks his promises, or redefines the recipients so he doesn't have to keep his promises?

The New Testament church is a new economy in God's management of his household affairs. It is a separate economy from gentile and Jew alike. Paul's argument is well stated: Christ created in himself one new people, the New Testament church, from two peoples, the Jew and gentile. Therefore the New Testament church is not a successor to Israel, does not surpass Israel, is not the continuation of Israel, but is something completely new in the history of God's relationship with humankind. Christ has reconciled both Jew and gentile in one body, Ephesians 2:16, and created a new body, "the household of God," 2:19, which is neither the household of Israel nor the household of paganism.

> Jew and gentile stand on the same level ground at the cross, equal to one another under God's Law of redemption and reconciliation. Therefore, each ceases to be gentile or Jew, each has been reconciled to God and to one another, and together they have become fellow-believers in Jesus Christ. They are a new man, not made out of the old stuff, but each made of new stuff. The believer in Jesus the Messiah, who was formerly Jew or gentile, but is now a new man in Christ Jesus, is brought near to the blessings of the covenants of promise, therefore brought near to one another. [Quiggle, *Ephesians*, 149.]

The New Testament church is not the caterpillar of Old Israel metamorphosed into the butterfly of a New Israel. The New Testament church was not formed from Judaism (Matthew 9:16–17) but is something newly revealed in the plans and processes of God. The Ephesian passage reveals the mystery of the church, not the exclusion of national ethnic Israel from eschatology. "A 'mystery' in Scripture is something which man is capable of knowing, but only when it has been revealed to him by God, and not through any searching of his own" [Trench, 55]. There are several mysteries in Scripture, of which three are important to eschatology.

> The mystery of the kingdom.

> The mystery of the rapture. (The rapture itself is not the mystery. The transformation and glorification of living saints is the mystery.)

> The mystery of the church.

The mystery of the church is exactly what Paul explains in Ephesians. First, people out of every nation, ethnicity, language, and tribe will be united spiritually by faith in Christ, so that worldly religious distinctions (Jew, pagan) no longer exist between saved people. Second, all those who are "in Christ," a term which describes the New Testament church, will share equally with national ethnic Israel certain future promises God made to national ethnic through the four covenants mentioned above. In other words, the New Testament church does not surpass Israel to become a New Israel, but participates in certain promises God made to national ethnic Israel.

This mystery of the church is hand-in-hand with Old Testament prophecies concerning the Davidic-Messianic Kingdom, wherein the gentiles are to participate with the Jews in that yet-future kingdom. The point here is that national ethnic Israel was not eliminated from God's plans by the dispensation of the New Testament church. Rather, a new people were created, a new people in the household of God.

Hebrews 3:1–6 tells us who is in the household of God. "Moses" is in the household, i.e., the people whom Moses represented, national ethnic Israel, are members of the house. Christ is in the house, i.e., the people whom Christ represents, the New Testament church, are members of the house. In actuality the house belongs to Christ, and in his house are many rooms wherein he has gathered distinct people groups which may be broadly described as pre-flood believers, post-flood believers, national ethnic Israel, and the New Testament church (and after the New Testament church, Tribulation and Kingdom believers).

The argument in Hebrews is, do not return to the Mosaic Law but press on to maturity on Christ. Therefore the Writer does not concern himself with believers living prior to the Mosaic covenant (with the exception of a few words about Abraham) but they too are part of the household. Our discussion of eschatology and the Kingdom must by necessity focus on Israel and the church, but God has an eschatological purpose and inheritance for those persons who were saved from Adam to Moses. The future is not as simplistic as the non-dispensationalist wishes it was. The infinitely complex God has a complex plan and processes which suit a complex purpose that encompass past, present, and eternity-future. If, as is the case, God has a separate program for people groups other than Israel and the church (e.g., holy angels, fallen angels, martyred Tribulation saints, living Tribulation saints, etc.), then is it irrational or unbelievable that he has a separate program for national ethnic Israel and a separate program for the New Testament church?

In this present dispensation of the New Testament church,

individual members of national ethnic Israel join the church by grace through faith just like any other person from any other people group. Just like saved gentiles cease to be pagans, even so saved Hebrews cease to be Jews (Jews: those who practice Judaism) to become Christians. The Hebrew in the New Testament church has not left one Israel to become part of another. He or she is a member of a separate and distinct group of saved peoples, the New Testament church. This new people group, the church, did not eliminate Israel or gentiles from eschatology. Nor was either people group replaced by the church.

Gentiles In The Davidic-Messianic Kingdom

The inclusion of gentiles in Israel's eschatology goes well-beyond the promise made through Abraham, Genesis 12:3. A few texts will make the point.

Micah 4:1–2, But in the latter days it shall come to pass, that the mountain of Jehovah's house shall be established on the top of the mountains, and it shall be exalted above the hills; and peoples shall flow unto it. 2 And many nations shall go and say, Come ye, and let us go up to the mountain of Jehovah, and to the house of the God of Jacob; and he will teach us of his ways, and we will walk in his paths (ASV).

Amos 9:11–12, In that day will I raise up the tabernacle of David that is fallen, and close up the breaches thereof; and I will raise up its ruins, and I will build it as in the days of old; 12 that they may possess the remnant of Edom, and all the nations that are called by my name, saith Jehovah that doeth this (ASV).

Zechariah 14:16, And it shall come to pass, that every one that is left of all the nations that came against Jerusalem shall go up from year to year to worship the King, Jehovah of hosts, and to keep the feast of tabernacles (ASV).

Psalms 2:7–8, I will tell of the decree: Jehovah said unto me, Thou art my son; this day have I begotten thee. 8 Ask of me, and I will give (thee) the nations for thine inheritance, and the uttermost parts of the earth for thy possession (ASV).

Psalm 47:8–9, God reigneth over the nations: God sitteth upon his holy throne. 9 The princes of the peoples are gathered together (to be) the people of the God of Abraham: for the shields of the earth belong unto God; He is greatly exalted (ASV).

Psalms 72:11, Yea, all kings shall fall down before him: all nations shall serve him (ASV).

Daniel 7:14, And to him [Christ] is given dominion, and glory, and a kingdom, and all peoples, nations, and languages do serve him, his dominion [is] a dominion age-during, that passeth not away, and his kingdom that which is not destroyed (YLT).

In the Old Testament context in which these texts were given by the Holy Spirit to the prophets, the "nations" and the "peoples" can only mean gentiles. Some would say that in this New Testament church dispensation there is no more Jew and gentile in a spiritual sense. That is nonsense. Outside the church, in the world, these distinctions continue. Within the church all saved persons are Christians but ethnic, racial, and national distinctions still exist, because the New Testament church is made up of believers from every nation, tribe, tongue, and people. However, those worldly distinctions become unimportant within the church, as Paul made clear in Galatians 3:28; Colossians 3:11, and in his letter to Philemon, recommending Philemon receive his runaway-now-returned property, Onesimus, as his Christian brother (see my commentary on Philemon). Within the church one is not slave or free, Jew or pagan, Hebrew or gentile, but is a Christian—one who worships Christ the Savior.

Outside the church worldly divisions persist and divide people. All gentiles who do not worship Jesus are spiritually pagans, existing as a people separate from the church. All Hebrews who do not worship Jesus are spiritually Jews, existing as a people separate from the church. When Christ returns there will be gentiles outside the church to be saved and receive the Old Testament promises, just as there will be Hebrews to be saved and receive the promises when the Lord returns to earth to receive his kingdom. The gentiles in the New Testament church have not "surpassed" the prophecies of the inclusion of gentiles in the Davidic-Messianic-Millennial kingdom. Christ himself said gentiles not part of the New Testament church will be part of his kingdom, Matthew 25:34, compare Zechariah 14:11.

Nor have the Hebrews been surpassed by the church. The Old

Testament verses given above are clear that gentiles will participate with national ethnic Israel in the kingdom. The New Testament clearly teaches that the church is not spiritual Israel, by using the terms "church" and "Israel" in an exclusive manner to indicate two separate peoples of God. Therefore, there remains an inheritance to the gentiles and to national ethnic Israel, which are the eschatological promises given through the Old Testament prophets. Verses such as Romans 2:28–29; 9:1–11:36; Galatians 3:17–19, 28–29 should be interpreted in the clear light of Paul's Ephesian explanation of the mystery of the church as a people group neither gentile nor Israel, and by the consistent and clear Scripture definition and use of the term Israel. As I have shown from Scripture, national ethnic Israel and the New Testament church are never confused. They are separate entities in the plan of God.

Fulfillment Of National Ethnic Israel's Covenants

The Abrahamic covenant was confirmed by the Land covenant, Deuteronomy 29:14–30:20 and the Davidic covenant, 2 Samuel 7:11b–17; 1 Chronicles 17:10b–15. The things promised in the Abrahamic covenant are presented in Genesis 12:1–3, 7; 13:14–17; 15:1–21; 17:1–21; 22:15–18. They pertain to Abraham personally and to Abraham's seed Israel and Christ, and through Christ to the gentiles.

The Mosaic covenant did not annul the Abrahamic covenant. Paul states this very clearly at Galatians 3:17. The Mosaic Law established the conditions whereby Israel would remain in the land and enjoy the blessings of the Abrahamic covenant. The blessings and curses of the Law indicate the Mosaic covenant was a conditional covenant that depended on the actions of the people for its fulfillment. Neither the Abrahamic covenant that preceded the Law, nor the Davidic covenant during the time of the law, contained the blessings and curses of the Mosaic Law, i.e., the Abrahamic and Davidic covenants did not depend on the people for their fulfillment. Moses distinguished the Mosaic and Abrahamic covenants, Deuteronomy 5:2–3.

The Writer of Hebrews, 8:13, said God had made a New covenant subsequent to the Mosaic Law, a covenant which made the Mosaic covenant obsolete, growing old, and ready to vanish. That "New" covenant, Jeremiah 31, was new to Israel in relation to the Mosaic Law, and is never set against the prior Abrahamic and Davidic, nor

Palestinian, covenants. YHWH distinctly stated the New covenant was "Not like the covenant that I made with their fathers, in the day of my laying hold on their hand, to bring them out of the land of Egypt," Jeremiah 31:32 (YLT). The New covenant is not fulfilled in the Law but in a change of the heart, i.e., the soul, something Israel knew:

> Deuteronomy 30:6, And YHWH your God will circumcise your heart, and the heart of your descendants, to love YHWH your God with all your heart, and with all your soul, for the sake of your life.

> Psalms 40:8, I delight to do your will, O my God; yes, your law is in my heart.

> Proverbs 3:1, My son, forget not my law, but allow your heart keep my commandments.

The New covenant was created by God's love for his people and is fulfilled in their love for God. The covenant, its benefits, and the people for whom it was made, are guaranteed by the order and stability of the universe [McClain, 159].

> Jeremiah 31:35–37, This is what the Lord says: The One who gives the sun for light by day, the fixed order of moon and stars for light by night, who stirs up the sea and makes its waves roar—the Lord of Hosts is His name: 36 If this fixed order departs from My presence—this is the Lord's declaration—then also Israel's descendants will cease to be a nation before Me forever. 37 This is what the Lord says: If the heavens above can be measured and the foundations of the earth below explored, I will reject all of Israel's descendants because of all they have done—this is the Lord's declaration (HCSB).

This declaration was made to national ethnic Israel, not to a people group—the New Testament church—which would not exist for another six hundred years. By the grace and purpose of God the New Testament church enjoys a New covenant in the death of Christ that has the same spiritual benefits of the New covenant YHWH made with national ethnic Israel, Ephesians 2:12–13, 19. The benefits the New Testament church now enjoys did not replace the New covenant YHWH made with national ethnic Israel through Jeremiah. The Writer of Hebrews (8:8–12; 10:16–17) does not say the New covenant was completely fulfilled by the New covenant for New Testament church. The New covenant for national ethnic Israel remains in force to be applied to national ethnic Israel when Christ returns.

According to the above quote from Jeremiah 31:35–37, the only way the New covenant will *not* be fulfilled toward the nation Israel is if the fixed order of the universe can be changed. That promise was made to living Israelis concerning their physical descendants. The New covenant has not been fulfilled toward their physical descendants as a nation (Jeremiah 31:31, 33, the "house of Israel"). Therefore there remains a yet-future fulfillment of the New covenant for national ethnic Israel. The scattered people of national ethnic Israel, Jeremiah 31:10, will be re-gathered from the ends of the earth, 31:8, to the physical land of Israel, 31:23–24 and experience the New covenant, 31:31–34. (ASV)

> Jeremiah 31:8, Behold, I will bring them from the north country, and gather them from the uttermost parts of the earth, (and) with them the blind and the lame, the woman with child and her that travaileth with child together: a great company shall they return hither.
>
> Jeremiah 31:10, Hear the word of Jehovah, O ye nations, and declare it in the isles afar off; and say, He that scattered Israel will gather him, and keep him, as a shepherd doth his flock.
>
> Jeremiah 31:23–24, Thus saith Jehovah of hosts, the God of Israel, Yet again shall they use this speech in the land of Judah and in the cities thereof, when I shall bring again their captivity: Jehovah bless thee, O habitation of righteousness, O mountain of holiness. 24 And Judah and all the cities thereof shall dwell therein together, the husbandmen, and they that go about with flocks.
>
> Jeremiah 31:31–34, Behold, the days come, saith Jehovah, that I will make a new covenant with the house of Israel, and with the house of Judah: 32 not according to the covenant that I made with their fathers in the day that I took them by the hand to bring them out of the land of Egypt; which my covenant they brake, although I was a husband unto them, saith Jehovah. 33 But this is the covenant that I will make with the house of Israel after those days, saith Jehovah: I will put my law in their inward parts, and in their heart will I write it; and I will be their God,

and they shall be my people: 34 and they shall teach no more every man his neighbor, and every man his brother, saying, Know Jehovah; for they shall all know me, from the least of them unto the greatest of them, saith Jehovah: for I will forgive their iniquity, and their sin will I remember no more.

And how secure are these promises YHWH made to national ethnic Israel? Re-read Jeremiah 31:35–37, quoted above.

Notice Jeremiah 31:31. God will make his New covenant with "the house of Israel" and "the house of Judah." At the time Jeremiah received this prophecy there was no house of Israel. Within Jeremiah's historical context the "house of Israel" referred to the northern kingdom of Israel-Samaria (the ten tribes excluding Judah and Benjamin) which had been conquered and dispersed by Assyria about one hundred years earlier (722 BC). Members of the tribes of Judah and Benjamin began their return to Palestine after the Babylonian captivity, circa 536 BC. The ten tribes have *never* returned as tribes, as a nation, although individuals out of these tribes have probably returned to the land. The ten tribes of Israel-Samaria remain to this day to be gathered out of the gentile nations where God scattered them; as do the tribes of Judah and Benjamin scattered in AD 70. Individuals have returned to form a nation, but the nation has not been returned by Christ sending his angels (Matthew 24:31) to gather all of national ethnic Israel from the lands to which they were scattered.

The promises and covenants God gave national ethnic Israel through Jeremiah have not, at this time, to this day, been fulfilled. Is the New Testament church a New Israel with exclusive rights to the promises and covenants? Has God lied to generations of Israelis since Jeremiah's prophecies—for the past 2,650 years (628 BC – AD 2022)? Or will God keep his promises and covenants to national ethnic Israel? The answer is,

If this fixed order [sun, moon, stars] departs from My presence—this is the Lord's declaration—then also Israel's descendants will cease to be a nation before Me forever . . . If the heavens above can be measured and the foundations of the earth below explored, I will reject all of Israel's descendants because of all they have done—this is the Lord's declaration (HCSB).

That fixed order of sun, moon, and stars will not be changed until after the second advent, after the Davidic-Messianic Kingdom, and after the Great White Throne judgment, when this present order is destroyed see 2 Peter 3:10; Revelation 20:11 ("the heaven and earth fled"), and a new heaven and earth are created, Revelation 21:1. Even in the new heaven and earth the distinction between national ethnic Israel and the New Testament church remains, Revelation 21:12, 14.

This also is what Paul believed, Romans 11:2, 26–27. God has not rejected national ethnic Israel and he has not broken his promises.

Returning to the Abrahamic covenant, when Paul in Galatians interpreted the blessing of Genesis 12:3, and the seed of 22:18, as meaning Christ, he was using an allegorical interpretation (the only time in Scripture). His interpretation applied the promises to Abraham's physical and spiritual descendants—Hebrews and gentiles—who have faith.

However, Paul's interpretation, and the Holy Spirit's application of the promises to individual Hebrews and gentiles, did not change or annul the original intent of the promises toward national ethnic Israel. Paul's allegorical interpretation is very specific: the Galatians did not need the Mosaic Law because through the seed (grammatically singular, meaning the Christ), they received the blessings of faith. In the original Old Testament context the word "seed" is a collective singular with reference to the nation Israel. To paraphrase Paul (Galatians 3:17) to the current argument, the promises made to the physical seed of Abraham, which is national ethnic Israel, were not annulled two thousand years later when the one seed, Christ, accomplished the fulfillment promised through the one seed.

The following are the covenant promises made to Abraham.

A national land: Genesis 12:1; 13:14–15, 17.

Redemption for Israel and the nations: Genesis 12:3; 22:18.

Numerous descendants to form a great nation: Genesis 12:2; 13:16; 17:2–6 ff.; 22:15–18.

Some of these applied to Abraham personally, some applied to Israel, some to all nations.

Abraham's name shall be great (personally)

A great nation will come from Abraham (Israel)

In Abraham all families of earth shall be blessed (nations)

The land of Palestine given to Abraham (personally) and his seed (Israel) forever.

The multitude of his seed as the dust of the earth (Israel)

The multitude of his seed as the stars in the sky (Israelis and gentiles saved by grace through faith in Christ)

Whoever blessed him should be blessed; whoever cursed him should be cursed (personally; Israel)

He should be the father of many nations (nations)

Kings should proceed from him (fulfilled to him through his descendants and through Christ.)

The land of Canaan to be an everlasting possession (Israel)

God will be a God to him and his seed (personally, Israel, nations)

His seed shall possess the gates of his enemies (Israel)

In his seed all nations of earth blessed (nations)

These are the fulfillments of those predictions, some in full, some now-yet future, some sequentially. All are unconditional.

Abraham blessed temporally: land (Genesis 13:14, 15, 17); servants (15:17 ff.); cattle, silver, gold (13:2; 24:34, 35).

Abraham blessed spiritually: happy life separated toward God (Genesis 13:8; 14:22, 23); communion with God (13:18; 18:17); consistent prayer life (28:23–33); sustained by God (21:22); peace confidence (22:5, 8, 10, 12, 16–18)

Abraham had a great name; was a channel of blessing to his household, posterity, world through the Savior (Galatians 3:8, 16)

Blessing & cursing of others (Genesis 14:12–16, 18–20; 20:2–18; 21:22–34; 23:1–20; Deuteronomy 30:7; Isaiah 14:1–2; Joel 3:1–8; Matthew 25:40-45.

Abraham had an heir, Genesis 21:2.

Father of many nations: Ishmael, Genesis 25:12–18; Keturah, 25:1–6; national ethnic Israel through Jacob-Israel.

The land: promised to Abraham: Genesis 15:18, from the River of Egypt to the Euphrates River. Partly fulfilled in David's and Solomon's kingdoms. Solomon's kingdom, 1 Kings 4:24, was from the Euphrates River to the *wādi* or brook of Egypt.

There is little argument from the non-dispensationalist that Abraham became great, that the nation Israel was born though his seed, and that all the families of earth are blessed in Christ. The sticking point of the non-dispensationalist's rejection of national ethnic Israel comes down to their restoration and possession of the land (after the second advent) in the Davidic-Messianic Kingdom (which most non-dispensationalists reject). The non-dispensationalist will say Israel possessed the land in Old Testament times, so there is no future fulfillment, and therefore this promise is not applicable to the New Testament church as the "New Israel." The dispensationalist says Israel will be re-gathered, restored, and possess the land promised to them through Abraham, because the land was never fully possessed under David and Solomon.

The land to be inherited and possessed by Israel was defined in the Abrahamic covenant as from the "River of Egypt" to the "River Euphrates," Genesis 15:18. Solomon's kingdom extended from the Euphrates in the north to *Wādi el 'Arish* in the south. This *wādi* or stream is also known as the Brook of Egypt, River of Egypt, or Torrent of Egypt, depending on the Bible version or Bible encyclopedia/dictionary consulted. The word translated "river" in both uses at Genesis 15:18 is the Hebrew *nāhār* [Harris, s. v. 1315a], river, stream. Outside of the Psalms, which use it as a simile, *nāhār* refers to major rivers. Harris says "*nāhār* does not seem to be applied to the Nile." However, in this instance it cannot be applied to the *wādi*. The use requires a parallel expression: the *nāhār* Euphrates forms the northern boundary of the land promised to Israel, and the *nāhār* of Egypt forms the southern boundary. The parallel requires a river equivalent to the Euphrates. That river is the Nile, the "River of Egypt."

The Old Testament has three defining uses of the phrase "river of Egypt," which confirm the river in view is the Nile. These are,

> Genesis 15:18, On the same day YHWH made a covenant with Abram, saying, "To your descendants I have given this land, from the River of Egypt to the great river, the River Euphrates."

Amos 8:8, Shall the land not tremble for this, and everyone mourn who dwells in it? All of it shall swell like the river, heave and subside like the River of Egypt.

Amos 9:5, The Lord YHWH of hosts, he who touches the earth and it melts, and all who dwell there mourn; all of it shall swell like the river, and subside like the River of Egypt.

To Abraham, when we consider his historical context, there was only one River of Egypt: the Nile. To Amos and his contemporaries the phrase "swell like the river" identified one river, the Nile, whose annual overflow fertilized and watered the farmlands along its banks. The annual flood and sinking of the Nile could cause great destruction to land and structures, and provided a simile for an earthquake in Amos 8:8; 9:5.

Moreover, the Hebrew word translated "river" is not the same word translated "brook." In Genesis 15:18 the word is *nāhār* [Harris, 1315a]. The parallel with "the great *nāhār*," which is always the Euphrates, requires the *nāhār* of Egypt to be a *nāhār* equal to the Euphrates. The River Nile satisfies the parallel. In Amos the word is *yeʾōr*, "river," which "usually refers to the Nile" [Harris, s. v. 832]. However, the word translated "brook" is *nahal,* a *wādi* [Harris, s. v. 1343a]. When speaking about the division of Palestine to the tribes of Israel, e.g., Numbers 34:5; Joshua 15:4, 47, the *nahal* of Egypt is *Wādi el ʾArish*.

In 1 Kings 4:24, the ancient historian states Solomon had dominion over all the river on this side of the *nāhār*, "the river," from Tiphsah even to Gaza. The *nāhār* here is the Euphrates, as indicated by the mention of the village of Tiphsah, which lay on the south bank of the Euphrates (at the great bend in the river east of modern day Aleppo, Syria) [Aharoni, plate 105]. The southern boundary of Solomon's kingdom, according to 1 Kings 4:24, was Gaza. If the ancient historian meant the Philistine city of Gaza, then *Wādi el ʾArish* is about twenty-five miles south of the city, forming the southern border between Solomon's Israel and Egypt. If the historian meant the Philistine territory of which Gaza was the capital, then from Solomon's time to the present-day, *Wādi el ʾArish* forms the border between Egypt and Gaza [Aharoni, plate 105]. Solomon's kingdom lay between the River Euphrates and the *Wādi el ʾArish*.

The River of Egypt in Genesis 15:18, is not *Wādi el ʾArish*, the Brook of Egypt, but is the River Nile. Israel never possessed all the land promised to Abraham, from the River Euphrates to the River Nile, so the promise remains to be fulfilled.

Moreover, Solomon's kingdom did not control all the land given to the twelve tribes. The land given to the tribe of Asher remained partly controlled by Pheonicia. The land given to the tribe of Judah remained partly controlled by Philistia. The Ammonites remained settled in the land given to Reuben. The promise remains to be fulfilled.

The promise of the land to national ethnic Israel was confirmed in the Land covenant, Deuteronomy 29:1–30:10.

Israel will disobey and be scattered, 29:2–30:1.

Israel will repent, 30:2.

Messiah will return, 30:3.

Israel will be re-gathered, 30:3–4.

Israel will possess the promised land, 30:5.

The enemies of Israel will be judged, 30:7.

Israel will receive full blessings, 30:8–10.

Some teach these things were fulfilled in the return from Babylon, and that there is no promise of a land to national ethnic Israel because no promises of possession were made after the Babylonian captivity (not true, see below). A few points will clarify this issue. One, God does not have to repeat himself, especially if the original promise has not been fulfilled. Two, the covenant states, "[YHWH will] gather you again from all the nations where YHWH your God has scattered you." This was not fulfilled. The Jews dispersed in the Assyrian captivity were not re-gathered into Israel to possess the land. As to the descendants of the Jews from the Babylonian captivity, more Jews remained in Persia than returned to Israel. The book of Esther takes place midway in chronology of the book of Ezra (between Ezra chapters 6 and 7). Esther's story makes clear Jews lived throughout the Persian kingdom.

The current occupation of the land, 1948–present, is not a fulfillment—there are more Jews outside Israel than in Israel. National ethnic Israel has never been re-gathered by YHWH, or Christ (Matthew 24:31) from *all* the nations where God scattered them. Additionally, the re-gathering is to occur *after* Messiah's advent. The re-gathering didn't occur during the first advent—just the opposite, Israel was scattered to the nations—so it must be waiting for the second.

It does no good to say that if the New Testament church is the New Israel, then God is re-gathering "Israel" through individual salvations. The church was never a people group located in one place which God then scattered as punishment for their disobedience. Christ is not re-gathering the church; he is saving sinners out of the world and placing them into the church. To say, as does Reformed theology, that God is re-gathering "Israel" through individual salvations, is to spiritualize a literal promise about a literal return of a literal people group, national ethnic Israel.

Moreover, the penultimate point of the covenant has not been fulfilled: the enemies have not been judged. The return from the Babylonian captivity was not a fulfillment of the covenant because the Jews remained—and still remain—under the control of the gentiles, Luke 21:24, until Christ returns.

Finally, the Jews are to be re-gathered to their land by the returning Messiah, Matthew 24:31; Mark 13:27, to take permanent possession of their land, Deuteronomy 30:8–10. The "elect" of the Matthew and Mark passages concern Israel, as Matthew 24:3, 15, indicate, and as Zephaniah 3:19; Zechariah 10:10; Ezekiel 36:24; Jeremiah 23:3; 29:14 and other Old Testament verses support.

Let us settle this issue of national ethnic Israel's possession of the land. Psalm 105:8 states YHWH remembers his covenant forever. Not "remembered," as though past and completed, but "remembers," because it is active and yet to be fully completed. Which covenant? The one made with Abraham and confirmed with Isaac and Jacob Psalm 105:9–10. How long will God remember this covenant? To a thousand generations, Psalm 105:8. A "thousand generations" is a hyperbolic way of saying forever. However, just for the sake of argument, how many generations have passed since the covenant was given to Abraham to the present time. The number of years in a generation is hotly debated, but let us take the lowest number proposed, twenty years. Rounding off the years from Abraham to now, about 4,000 years have passed since God gave the covenant to Abraham. So 4,000 years divided by twenty years in a generation means so far about two hundred generations have passed. God continues to remember his covenant with Abraham, Isaac, and Jacob, it will be literally fulfilled.

YHWH's covenant with Abraham, the covenant YHWH confirmed with Isaac and Jacob, encompassed many promises, as we have seen. Which promise does the Psalmist—under the superintending inspiration of the Holy Spirit—single out that God remembers to a thousand generations? Psalm 105:11, "I will give to you the land of Canaan as the portion of your inheritance." In 105:13–45 the Psalmist recalls a specific example of YHWH remembering his covenant. In the time of Moses YHWH "remembered his holy promise to Abraham . . . and gave them the lands of the gentiles."

After the Babylonian captivity YHWH remembered his holy promise and gave his people the land. And after being scattered throughout the world for almost 1,900 years (AD 70–1948) YHWH remembered and gave his people the land. YHWH remembers his covenant to a thousand generations. As discussed above, national ethnic Israel has not yet fully possessed the land from the Euphrates to the Nile, so YHWH will remember his covenant and give the nation the land, even as confirmed by the Palestinian covenant, Deuteronomy 29:1–30:10. YHWH's covenant with Abraham to give national ethnic Israel the land is an everlasting covenant which will be fulfilled even if it takes a thousand generations.

The Restoration Of National Ethnic Israel

Some will say that the promises concerning the restoration of national ethnic Israel to the land (the re-gathering) were fulfilled when Israel returned from Babylon, and there was never a prophecy made, never a promise given, concerning the Jews being brought into the land again. If God did not make additional prophecies it would not be relevant, for his word stands sure until it is fulfilled. But in fact, God did make prophecy and promises of restoration to the land *after* the Babylonian return. Zechariah, Haggai, Malachi, and parts of Daniel were written after the return from Babylon. The Babylonian exiles' return to Israel took place 538 BC (under Zerubbabel), 458 BC (under Ezra), and 444 BC (Nehemiah). Daniel was written circa 605–536 BC; Zechariah circa 520–490 BC; Haggai circa 520–505 BC; Malachi circa 435–400 BC.

In the book of Zechariah (NKJV):

2:10–12. Sing and rejoice, O daughter of Zion! For behold, I am coming and I will dwell in your midst, says YHWH. Many nations shall be joined to YHWH in that day, and they shall become my people. And I will dwell in your midst. Then you will know that YHWH of hosts has sent me to you. And YHWH will take possession of Judah as his inheritance in the holy land, and will again choose Jerusalem.

8:7–8, Thus says YHWH of hosts: Behold, I will save my people from the land of the east and from the land of the west; I will bring them back, and they shall dwell in the midst of Jerusalem. They shall be my people and I will be their God in truth and righteousness.

12:10, And I will pour on the house of David and on the inhabitants of Jerusalem the Spirit of grace and supplication; then they will look on me whom they pierced. Yes, they will mourn for him as one mourns for his only son, and grieve for him as one grieves for a firstborn. [This refers to a time after the crucifixion. It didn't happen then and it hasn't happened yet.]

14:1–5, Behold, the day of YHWH is coming, and your spoil will be divided in your midst. For I will gather all the nations to battle against Jerusalem; the city shall be taken, the houses rifled, and the women ravished. Half of the city shall go into captivity, but the remnant of the people shall not be cut off from the city. Then YHWH will go forth and fight against those nations, as he fights in the day of battle. And in that day his feet will stand on the Mount of Olives, which faces Jerusalem on the east. And the Mount of Olives shall be split in two, from east to west, making a very large valley; half of the mountain shall move toward the north and half of it toward the south. Then you shall flee through my mountain valley, for the mountain valley shall reach to Azal. Yes, you shall flee as you fled from the earthquake in the days of Uzziah king of Judah. Thus YHWH my God will come, and all the saints with you. [The last sentence coordinates with Revelation 19:11–14.]

14:9–11, In that day [an eschatological term] it shall be 'YHWH is one,' and his name one. All the land shall be turned into a plain from Geba to Rimmon south of Jerusalem. Jerusalem shall be raised up and inhabited in her place from Benjamin's Gate to the place of the First Gate and the Corner Gate, and from the Tower of Hananel to the king's winepresses. The people shall dwell in it; and no longer shall there be utter destruction, but Jerusalem shall be safely inhabited."

14:16, And it shall come to pass that everyone who is left of all the nations which came against Jerusalem shall go up from year to year to worship the King, YHWH of hosts, and to keep the Feast of Tabernacles. [Since this prophecy has not been fulfilled, it also indicates a restoration to the land, other than the Babylonian restoration.]

So we see that prophecies of national ethnic Israel returning to the land were made after the Babylonian captivity, prophecies which address re-gathering the nation Israel into the land. In addition to those in Zechariah, Haggai 2:6–7 is a part of the re-gathering promise since this prophecy is yet to be fulfilled; Malachi 4:1–3 has yet to occur and requires the re-gathering.

Haggai 2:6–7 reads,

For thus says YHWH Sabaoth. "Yet once more—it is a little—I will shake the heavens , and the earth, and the sea, and the dry land, and I will shake all nations, and shall come the treasure of all nations, and I will fill this house with glory," says YHWH Sabaoth.

In the historical context, God, through the prophet, is encouraging the people to complete the restoration of the temple, which they did in 516 BC. To those who heard Haggai, the prophecy meant God would honor their restored temple, though it was less than the old temple Solomon had built. God will fill "this latter temple" (2:9) with glory after he shakes the world and the treasures of all nations will fill the temple. There will be a restored temple when Christ returns, Revelation 11:1–2; 2 Thessalonians 2:4. A restored temple assumes a restored nation. Considering the temple waits to be restored, the fulfillment is yet-future. God did not "shake the heavens and earth, sea and dry land" when the old temple was restored, 516 BC. Therefore, this prophecy remains to be completely fulfilled.

Malachi 4:1–3 speaks of the Tribulation period. It is a day that is coming: a far-future day. It is a day of destruction: the far-future

Tribulation. "But for you who fear my name" it is a day when Christ, "the Sun of Righteousness," will return with healing in his wings. Who will he heal? The far-future descendants of those persons Malachi the Israeli prophet is addressing: national ethnic Israel.

Daniel 12:1 reveals the restoration of national ethnic Israel. In this Old Testament text a reference to the "nation" can only be a reference to national ethnic Israel. The angel is speaking to an Israeli about his people Israel. Promises are made to Daniel concerning the far-future of the nation he belongs to by birth. The angel Michael will "stand up" for national ethnic Israel, because he is the great archangel who watches over and defends the nation.

Michael will stand up for Israel during a time to trouble such as has never been experienced by national ethnic Israel from the time they became a nation in the land of Egypt. This is the Tribulation, described in similar terms in the gospels, e.g., Matthew 24:21. At that time, said the angel to Daniel, "your people" shall be delivered, everyone written in the book. The book of life isn't just for the New Testament church. The book of life records the name of every citizen of heaven from Adam forward. We know this because the book of life is at the GWT judgment to validate that none of those present—the unsaved from the beginning of the world—are saved. So the saved of national ethnic Israel are in the book. The reference to "your people" confirms national ethnic Israel is in view. These are Daniel's people, which means they are Israelis.

Another angel, Gabriel, used the exact same term "your people" in Daniel 9:24. There Gabriel is beginning a prophecy concerning "your people and your holy city." Who is the angel speaking to? Daniel, a national ethnic Israeli; see 9:22. The title, "your people" means national ethnic Israel.

Between the restoration of national ethnic Israel in Daniel 12:1 and the resurrections in 12:2–3 is a conjunction, "and." National ethnic Israel will be delivered in the Tribulation (no specific timing is given) *and* those of national ethnic Israel who "sleep in the dust," i.e., are physically dead, will be resurrected. In 12:1–3 both living and physically dead Israelis are in view. The living to be rescued in the Tribulation and restored as a nation; the physically dead to be resurrected (no timing is given). There is a re-gathering and restoration for national ethnic Israel at the second advent.

When will the re-gathering and restoration occur? Other verses tell us that believers in the Tribulation are delivered at the second advent of Christ. When Christ returns at his second advent he will rescue his people, destroy his enemies, establish his kingdom, and reward his people with their inheritance, including a re-gathered national ethnic Israel.

Is there a confirmation of re-gathering and restoration? Yes, Daniel 12:13, where the prophet is told he will be resurrected to his lot/portion/inheritance at the end of the days. The prophecy doesn't just refer to Daniel, but to the nation Daniel represents, "your people." The portion (lot, inheritance) specifically refers to the portion of the land every Israelite had as a possession in the land of the covenant, from the Nile to the Euphrates, guaranteed through the Abrahamic and Land covenants, and secured in the Messiah as the eschatological hope of national ethnic Israel. God will not abandon his people Israel, but will fulfill the promises made to them in the covenants and confirmed to them through their prophets.

National Ethnic Israel Is Always Separate And Distinct

There is another truth that teaches God has a continuing program for national ethnic Israel, a program separate and distinct from his program for the New Testament church. That truth is that Israel is to remain a distinct national entity until the Christ comes again, even though dispersed throughout the world. There were to be three captivities or dispersions among the gentiles and three restorations.

1. The Egyptian bondage, Genesis 15:13–14.

> Restoration under the leadership of Moses and Joshua, Genesis 15; Joshua 1:2–7.

2. The Assyrian and Babylonian Captivities, Jeremiah 25:11–12.

> Restoration of the Babylonian captives only, Daniel 9:2; Jeremiah 25:11–12, under Zerubbabel son of Shealtiel and Joshua son of Jehozadak, Ezra 2:2; 3:8; and Ezra the scribe and Nehemiah, Ezra 7:11, 28; Nehemiah 2:5–9.

3. Among the nations, Deuteronomy 28:63–68, with 30:1–3, which occurred in AD 70 with the dissolution of the nation by the Romans.

> Restoration of the twelve tribes (national ethnic Israel) by Messiah at the second advent, Deuteronomy 30:3; Isaiah 66:22; Jeremiah 23:5–8; 31:36–37; Ezekiel 16:60–63; 37:21–25; Matthew 24:34; Acts 15:14–17.

Three dispersions and two restorations have been accomplished. The third dispersion occurred AD 70, but the restoration has not occurred. It has not occurred because,

> God did not cause the present re-gathering per Old and New Testament prophecies, e.g., Ezekiel 20:34; Matthew 24:31.

> All the Jews were not gathered from all the nations where God had scattered them in 722 BC (Assyrian Captivity), in 606 BC (Babylonian Captivity), and in AD 70 (dissolution of the nation).

> Neither the returns from the Babylonian captivity in 538, 458, and 444 BC, nor the current occupation from AD 1948–to present, by a small number of Jews, fulfilled the covenant and prophecy requiring all Israelis to be returned to the land.

> Wherever members of national ethnic Israel are living, Israel remains a distinct national entity despite dispersions: Jeremiah 31:3, 36; 33:15–17; Daniel 12:13; Isaiah 66:8, 20–23.

> There is the promise of the land: Genesis 15–18; Deuteronomy 28–30. The land was deeded to Abraham personally and is the legal inheritance of his physical posterity.

> There is the promise of Israel's future repentance: Deuteronomy 30:1–3; Isaiah 61:2–3; Zechariah 12:10; Matthew 5:4; 24:30.

> There is the promise of Israel's restoration: Deuteronomy 30:3–6; Acts 15:16–17; Amos 9:9–15.

The point of the arguments in this section was not to present a complete theology of Israel, but to indicate the following.

> The New Testament Church is not Israel, does not surpass Israel, is not a continuation of Israel.

> The New Testament church is not the fulfillment of promises made to Israel, although it does participate in a partial fulfillment of the New covenant, and will participate in other promises when they are fulfilled in national ethnic Israel,

Ephesians 2:12–13.

The New Testament church does not completely fulfill prophecies made to national ethnic Israel in either a literal or non-literal manner.

There are prophecies relevant to national ethnic Israel that have not been fulfilled but will be fulfilled for national ethnic Israel.

National ethnic Israel is promised to remain a distinct nation while dispersed among the nations.

When Messiah returns all national ethnic Israel is to be re-gathered from the nations where God has scattered them.

When Messiah returns all national ethnic Israel is to be restored to the land.

Final Arguments

There is a far-future eschatological event that reveals God intends Israel to be always a separate people group from the church. After the church dispensation, after the Tribulation period, after the Davidic-Messianic-Millennial Kingdom, God destroys the current heavens and earth, 2 Peter 3:10; Revelation 20:11, and then after the Great White Throne judgment of the unsaved, Revelation 20:12–15 God makes a new heaven and earth, Revelation 21:1. On that new earth God places the New Jerusalem, the eternal home of the saved from all dispensations past, 21:3. That city is built on twelve foundations, and on these foundations will be the names of the twelve apostles and Jesus the Christ, 21:14. Built into the walls of that city are twelve gates. There are names written on the gates: the names of the twelve tribes of the children of Israel, 21:12. In the purpose of God the New Testament church and national ethnic Israel are eternally separate people groups, always linked together, but with separate purposes in the plans and processes of God.

Let us permanently resolve this issue. At Isaiah 66:22 God has this to say about national ethnic Israel.

Says YHWH, Even as the new heavens and the new earth I will make will remain before me, so shall your descendants and your name remain.

To whom is YHWH speaking? None other than national ethnic

Israel. He does speak of the New Testament church at 65:1, but they are spoken of as a people group separate and distinct from national ethnic Israel; otherwise the verses following have no rational sense.

Paul understood this. He quoted Isaiah 65:1–2 at Romans 10:20–21, making the same distinction between Israel and the new people group, the New Testament church, that Isaiah made. If one continues through 66:24 it is obvious the people under discussion are national ethnic Israel. YHWH speaks of the "descendants of Jacob," 65:9; of "my holy mountain," and Jerusalem, 65:11, 18, 19; 66:10, 13. YHWH speaks of Zion, 66:8, in a context, 66:7–11, that refers to re-gathered Israel, compare Zechariah 10:6–10; 13:1. See also Jeremiah 33:19–22 where God says that his covenant with David—that he would have a son to reign on his throne—is as certain as God's covenant "with the day . . . with the night," a reference to the Noahic covenant, Genesis 8:22. In Jeremiah 33:23–26, God makes the same "day and night" pledge, saying he will not cast away the descendants of Jacob and David . . . the descendants of Abraham, Isaac, and Jacob, but he will cause them to return.

Returning to Isaiah 66:22, YHWH states national ethnic Israel is as permanent in the purpose of God as the new heavens and earth he will create. YHWH alluded to this same truth at 51:16. At 65:17 YHWH said he would create a new heavens and new earth, in which would be a new Jerusalem, wherein there would be joy but never weeping or crying. That sounds like the things God said in Revelation 21 about a new Jerusalem in which, 21:4, there is no death, no sorrow, no crying, and no pain because, Isaiah 65:17, 'the former will not be remembered or come to mind," and Revelation 21:4, "the former things have passed away."

Therefore, at Isaiah 66:22, God is speaking of national ethnic Israel, using the permanence of the new heavens and earth he will create as the assurance that the existence of national ethnic Israel—"your descendants and your name"—is as permanent as the new heavens and earth which God will make, Revelation 21:1.

Based on this declaration one can conclude that the New Testament church has not surpassed or replaced Israel, nor has it evolved into a new Israel. Contrary to non-dispensational theology, the New Testament church *is not* Israel in a newly reformed and expanded phase of existence, the church *is not* the continuation of Israel. As Scripture repeatedly asserts and confirms, national ethnic Israel and the New Testament church are separate people groups in God's purposes, plans, and processes. The New Testament church is not the New Israel.

Therefore, there is a New Testament church that is distinct from national ethnic Israel, and therefore there will be a rapture for the New Testament church, and there will be a Tribulation for national ethnic Israel and the rest of the earth dwellers, and there will be a Davidic-Messianic-Millennial Kingdom in which Christ will rule over this present earth.

First Thessalonians 4:13–18

Paul's first letter to the Thessalonians contains two passages that interact with the doctrine of the rapture. The first passage is 1 Thessalonians 4:13–18. The following is my exegesis of that passage from my book. *A Private Commentary on the Bible: Thessalonians*, beginning on page 119, lightly edited to the present purpose.

Introduction

Paul comes to this important piece of instruction as though he had not mentioned it during his time at Thessalonica. Yet, at 2 Thessalonians 2:5 Paul says he had told them these things while he was with them, see 2:1. Timothy's report, 1 Thessalonians 3:6, must have spoken of doubts, or perhaps confusion, by some. This is often the case with young Christians. When something is first explained, they think they understand. But upon further reflection, and the fact memory almost never remembers everything, they begin to have doubts, or have forgotten this or that detail. So Paul, the ever-patient teacher, explains again, perhaps (probably) giving more detail.

This passage is known to many as the "rapture" of the New Testament church. The word English word "rapture" is a transliteration of (a grammatical form of) the Latin word *rapiō*, which in English means "caught up. This Latin word was used in the Vulgate (Latin) version of 1 Thessalonians 4:17 to translate the Greek word *harpázō*, which means "caught up." "Then we the living remaining, together with them, will be *harpázō* in the clouds for the meeting of the Lord in the air"

The rapture is a yet-future event when physically living believers will be transformed and glorified (cf. 1 Corinthians 15:50–52), and then caught up at the command of Christ away from earth into the spirit domain to live with Christ eternally. Raptured believers will not experience physical death. At the moment of being caught up both soul and body of the physically living believer will be glorified to be free from the presence of sin and transformed to be incorruptible (respectively), and the New Testament believer will live endlessly in that continuous incorruptible state of body and soul.

As part of the rapture event, those believers previously dead, and even now residing in heaven as immaterial souls, will be rejoined with their resurrected bodies, transformed and glorified, to join with the raptured living believers. I will discuss these things, below, at the appropriate verse.

Translation 1 Thessalonians 4:13

Now we do not want you to be ignorant, brothers, about those having fallen asleep, so that you should not be grieved, even just as the rest—those not having hope.

EXPOSITION

In today's world the word "ignorant" is often confused with stupid. To be "stupid" is to be unable to learn, comprehend, or understand. To be "ignorant" is to not know, but to have the capacity to learn, and thereby come to know, comprehend, and understand. The Greek word here, *agnoeó* [Zodhiates, s. v. "50"], is formed from *noeó*, "to perceive," and the alpha privative "a," indicating "not," and thus means "to not know."

Paul says, "We do not want you not to know, brothers, about those having fallen asleep." Positively, he wants them to know about "those having fallen asleep." The 4:13–18 context indicates "asleep" is a euphemism for physical death: those believers who are currently with Jesus—the ones he is bringing with him from heaven, v. 14— are those who have "fallen asleep," which is to say, have physically died and are alive and living in heaven as immaterial souls.

The word translated "asleep" is *koimáō* [Zodhiates, s. v. "2837"], used for natural sleep. The word is used 18 times in the New Testament. Figuratively *koimáō* is used as a euphemism for physical death. Jesus defines this use for us, John 11:11–14.

> Jesus said: "Lazarus our friend has fallen asleep, but I go that I might awaken him.
>
> Disciples: "Master, if he has fallen asleep he will get well."
>
> Jesus: Then therefore Jesus plainly said to them, "Lazarus has died."

The sequel, as is well known, is Jesus went to resurrect Lazarus from the state of physical death.

The New Testament writers use *koimáō* in the sense of physical death. The first use of sleep as a euphemism for physical death is

Matthew 27:52. "many bodies of the saints having fallen asleep arose." They were dead; they experienced resurrection. See also Acts 7:60, the death of Stephen; Acts 13:36, the death of King David; 1 Corinthians 11:30; 15:6, 18, 21; 1 Thessalonians 4:13–15; 2 New Testament believers who have physically died; 2 Peter 3:4, Old Testament believers who physically died. At 1 Corinthians 15:20 Christ is risen out from the dead and is the firstfruits of those that sleep.

Scripture uses sleep as a euphemism for physical death because making an analogy between a body asleep and a body dead. Just as "the sleeper does not cease to exist while his body sleeps" [Vine, 95] even so the person continues to exist when absent from the body. Just as sleep is temporary, so the absence of the person from the body is temporary. "Sleep has its waking, death will have its resurrection" [Vine, 95].

A person is the union of material body and immaterial soul. Genesis 2:7 teaches the material body is animated by the presence of the immaterial soul. The immaterial soul is the person. Adam became a living being when the immaterial Adam, the soul, was joined with the inert physical body. Physical death is when the soul, the person, leaves the body to continue existing as a disembodied soul, until resurrection rejoins the person with the physical body.

> The soul is an immaterial substance that gives life and governs behavior in all living things. The soul is composed of the animating principle life and that complex of attributes which synergistically determine the nature and personality of living beings. The soul in humankind acts in three ways: the soul is the vital principle that animates the physical part of man's being; the soul is the person (the personality); the soul communes with God (through its faculty of spiritual perception). [Quiggle, *Dictionary.*]

Physical death is when the soul leaves the body. The physical death of the body is likened to sleep because the soul, the person, continues to exist alive, awake, and living his or her life after physical death. The Scripture never presents the dissolution of the soul as it does the body in physical death. The soul, once formed in the womb at conception, is immortal and always conscious. At physical death the person remains alive and conscious, not asleep or unconscious.

When absent from the physical body, what form does the soul possess? Disembodied souls have a form or "body" suited for life in the spirit domain. A created being always has a defined location in time and space, because he/she is a finite, limited being—unlike God who has no limits or definition to his essence. What to call the defined presence of the immaterial human soul when separated by physical death from the material body? There does not seem to be a better word than a "body" suited for life in the spirit domain. (So also the angels are finite beings defined by a location in time and space.)

The soul does not sleep between physical death and resurrection. So Paul in 2 Corinthians.

> 2 Corinthians 5:6 (HCSB), "while we are at home in the body we are away from the Lord.
>
> 2 Corinthians 5:8 (HCSB), yet we are confident and satisfied to be out of the body and at home with the Lord.

And at Philippians 1:23–24, "I am constrained between the two, having the desire to depart and to be with Christ, for that is much better; but to remain in the flesh is necessary for your sake."

This agrees with Paul in 1 Thessalonians 4:14, "Because if we believe that Jesus died and rose again, so also God will bring with him those having fallen asleep through Jesus." Which is to say, when Jesus returns, he will bring with him all those New Testament believers who have physically died prior to the rapture of the New Testament church, who have been living with Jesus in heaven.

Summarizing: home in the body, absent from the Lord; absent from the body, in the presence of the Lord. The physically dead believer is alive with Christ in heaven and returning with the Christ at the rapture.

For this reason, no believer should be grieved or lose hope when a fellow believer physically dies. The believer lives, even though the body has physically died. When the believer's soul departs his/her body (that departure is physical death) he/she immediately goes into the Lord's presence in heaven.

> When we [believers in Christ as Savior] close our eyes in death, we do not cease to be alive; rather, we experience a continuation of personal consciousness. No person is more

conscious, more aware, and more alert than when he passes through the veil from this world into the next. Far from falling asleep, we are awakened to glory in all of its significance. For the believer, death does not have the last word. Death has surrendered to the conquering power of the One who was resurrected as the firstborn of many brethren. [Sproul, article, *Death.*]

Human life begins at conception, and never ends. The body experiences a temporary cessation of life, known as physical death, but the person continues, to be reunited to his or her body in that act of God known as resurrection, to experience endless life in body and soul. Where a person continues after physical life and in the afterlife has always been the most important question of this mortal life. For the believer, the answer is, "With Christ." [Quiggle, *Life, Death, Eternity.*]

Translation 1 Thessalonians 4:14

Because if we believe that Jesus died and rose again, so also God will bring with him those having fallen asleep through Jesus.

EXPOSITION

The physical death and resurrection of Jesus the Christ is one of the essential doctrines of the Christian faith. Therefore, let me answer two questions. How may we be certain Jesus died physically? How may we be certain Jesus resurrected?

Jesus Died Physically

[Extract from Quiggle, *God Became Incarnate*, 151–153.]

Skeptics doubt Jesus' physical death, stating that he merely fainted on the cross and revived in the coolness of the tomb. Such opinions show a gross ignorance of the facts.

The Roman soldiers were masters of death. As in any military unit they had dealt death on the battlefield—not long distance as is done today, but face to face with a sword or spear. Each member of the Jerusalem unit was experienced at recognizing death. As in any military unit the crucifixion detail would have been a rotating duty performed by every member of the unit, so each was experienced at recognizing death by crucifixion. One of the soldiers, seeing that Jesus was dead,

John 19:33 (compare Matthew 27:54; Mark 15:44–45; Luke 23:47), stabbed the body through the heart with a spear. Why did he do this if he knew Jesus was dead? In the Roman military the soldiers responsible for the execution would suffer the penalty of the condemned if they allowed the condemned to escape. The soldier wanted to make sure there was no mistake. Out of a strong sense of self-preservation he stabbed Jesus through the heart to make sure his initial evaluation was correct: Jesus was dead.

Jesus' state of death was confirmed to Pilate by the Centurion in charge, Mark 15:44. Not merely that Jesus was dead, but that "he had been dead for some time." The recognition of his death, the assurance of his death, the passing of time from his death, and stabbing Jesus in the heart after his death assured the Roman Centurion and Pilate that Jesus had died. They knew their business better than skeptics and critics.

Jesus' enemies also knew he was dead. In the ancient world people died at home, in the streets, on the battlefield, and at places of execution. Everyone from childhood to old age knew and recognized the state of death, for they saw death face to face in their daily experiences. Jesus' enemies went to Pilate to ask for guards for the tomb, saying, Matthew 27:63, "we remember while he was still alive," indicating their knowledge that Jesus was dead. They had watched him die on the cross. They had seen the soldier stab Jesus through the heart. They asked Pilate for guards to prevent Jesus' disciples from stealing his dead body, thereby claiming a resurrection from the dead. Never mind that Jesus' followers were too frightened, discouraged, and disorganized to steal the body. The chief priests and Pharisees knew Jesus was dead and wanted everyone to remember him as he was: physically dead.

The tomb was closed, the entrance was blocked by a large stone, and the tomb was guarded by Roman soldiers, Matthew 28:65–66. Jesus resurrected and left without their knowledge. Angels came and rolled the stone away from the tomb; the soldiers trembled for fear and became comatose because of their fright. When they had recovered, they knew what would happen to them should it be reported to Pilate that Jesus' body was missing from the tomb: they would be executed. So they told the priests, who guaranteed their security should Pilate hear of this, and took money to lie about Jesus.

Jesus' dead body was wrapped in linen cloth, spices, and aromatic gums, Matthew 27:59; Mark 15:46; Luke 23:53. John 19:39–40 says he was wrapped in strips of linen cloth with about seventy-five pounds (100 *lítras*) of myrrh and aloes, with spices. He wasn't wrapped in a shroud, he was wrapped in *keiría*, strips of cloth, with a *soudárium*, a piece of cloth like a handkerchief [cf. Bromiley, *Encyclopedia*, s. v. "Burial"], "as the custom of the Jews is to bury" (NKJV).

Myrrh was an exuded gum from a tree which could be dried to a solid resin and, among other uses, was used for embalming. The body was wrapped in multiple layers of linen strips of cloth. Each layer was coated with the myrrh, aloes, and spices. As these dried the cloth was hardened by the dried resin of the myrrh. No one so embalmed could have wriggled out of the hardened cloths, compare John 11:44. The resurrected Jesus rose out of the cloths without disturbing them, John 20:6, in the same manner as he suddenly appeared in the upper room, John 20:19, 26, the doors being shut.

Consider the testimony of the two men who embalmed Jesus. Nicodemus and Joseph knew Jesus was dead, John 19:38–42. Death was a constant presence in the ancient world. There were no hospices, no hospitals, no funeral homes, no cremation societies. Family, relatives, and friends buried their dead. They knew a dead body when they saw one. Jesus died about 3:00 p.m. Sunset was about 6:00 p.m. Washing the body (the Jewish custom) and then embalming the body with layer upon layer of linen strips and myrrh and aloes and spices would have taken more than an hour. If Jesus had merely fainted, then the constant handling required to wash and wrap the body would have revived him. Jesus was physically dead. The soldiers knew he was dead, his enemies knew he was dead, and his friends knew he was dead.

Scripture states the death of Jesus in the plainest terms. Matthew 27:50, Jesus yielded up his spirit. Mark 15:37, Jesus breathed his last. Luke 23:46, Jesus breathed his last. John 19:30, Jesus gave up his spirit. He died physically, fully satisfying the physical penalty for sin. [Source: Quiggle, *God Became Incarnate*, 151–153.]

Jesus Resurrected

The Scripture is replete with eyewitness evidence Jesus

experienced resurrection. On Sunday, three days after his burial on Friday, Jesus appeared to several people.

To Mary Magdalene. John 20:14–18; Mark 16:9.

To the company of women who are returning to the sepulcher, Matthew 28:9 ff.

To the two disciples on the way to Emmaus. Luke 24:13 ff.; Mark 16:12.

To Peter. Luke 24:34; 1 Corinthians 15:5.

To the eleven and others. Luke 24:36 ff.; Mark 16:14; John 20:19 ff.

He was seen after the resurrection

To seven apostles at the Sea of Galilee, John 21:1.

To eleven disciples and others (1 Corinthians 15:6), in Galilee, Matthew 28:16–20.

To James, then the twelve, 1 Corinthians 15:5.

At the Ascension, Mark 16:15 ff.; Luke 24:50–53; Acts 1:4–9.

The historical fact of the resurrection is well-established by Scripture. His resurrection three days after physical death was the "proof of payment" that revealed Christ did make a propitiation for sin to God. For if he had not resurrected then he had not paid the sin debt in full. When Christ's saved people are resurrected to eternal life their resurrection will be because Christ made a propitiation for their sins on their behalf, his merit having been applied to remit their sin by their faith and his grace.

Paul said at 1 Corinthians 15:17, 19 that if Christ had not resurrected, then sins could not be forgiven, faith in Christ would be without purpose, and those who have faith in Christ would be "of all persons the most pitiable." But Jesus the Christ did resurrect out from among the dead.

Therefore, because Jesus resurrected, he will resurrect his saved people. Because he will resurrect his saved people, he will bring his saved people with him when he comes to the air to snatch away (rapture) the living church out of the world. We believe "Jesus died and rose again." Therefore, we believe "God will bring with him those having fallen asleep through Jesus."

Returning to the exposition.

The phrasing "God will bring with him those having fallen asleep through Jesus" is not quite what we, reading at such a distance in time from the first readers, might have expected. We might have expected, "Jesus will bring with him those having fallen asleep through him." What must always be born in mind is that biblical eschatology is kingdom eschatology. The goal of all the Old Testament and New Testament eschatology that looks toward Christ's return is in one way or another related to the coming Davidic-Messianic-Millennial Kingdom (2 Samuel 7:13, 16; Psalm 2). The rapture of the New Testament church is the event that begins the fulfillment of that kingdom prophecy, for the eschatological event after the rapture is the Tribulation, and then the second advent, and then the Davidic-Messianic-Millennial Kingdom.

Christ is right now "sat down at the right hand of God, hence forward expecting until his enemies may be placed as a footstool for his feet," Hebrews 10:12b–13. This prophecy about the kingdom began in the Old Testament, e.g., Psalm 110:1 (NKJV), "YHWH said to my Lord, sit at my right hand till I make your enemies your footstool." The kingdom is to be given to Christ by the Father.

Therefore it is the Father who begins the final events of the Day of the Lord, it is the Father who initiates that day by sending Christ to first take his church out of the world. The Father works his will in the world through the Son, and the Father and Son work their will in the world through the Holy Spirit. Therefore God—Father-Son-Spirit—will bring with him those having fallen asleep through Jesus. The God-man, Jesus the Christ, will bring with him those having fallen asleep through him.

A few commentators have problems with "those having fallen asleep through him," but the phrase means neither more nor less than the physical death of the New Testament saved in Christ. Christ will come to rapture his physically alive New Testament church by bringing with him the souls of those physically dead who are the saved of the New Testament church, those who have physically died between the AD 33 day of Pentecost and the unknown day of the rapture. The living will be transformed, the physically dead will be resurrected.

Translation 1 Thessalonians 4:15

For this we declare to you by the word of the Lord, that we the living remaining unto the coming of the Lord, shall never no never precede those having fallen asleep.

EXPOSITION

For this we declare to you by the word of the Lord

Paul gives to the Thessalonians (and to you and me), the revelation he received from Jesus concerning the rapture of the New Testament church, which revelation extends to 4:17. Now we should take care we do not disparage all else Paul has said just because he did not preface it with, "this we declare to you by the word of the Lord." All that Paul has written, in all of his letters, and all he said that is recorded in the Acts, was inspired by the Holy Spirit.

The practical meaning of "inspiration" is the accuracy, credibility, and authenticity of what is recorded in the Scripture. Paul gives this preface, "this we declare to you by the word of the Lord," for the same reason he said at, Galatians 1:12, I neither received the gospel from man, nor was I taught the gospel, but the gospel I preach is by revelation from Jesus Christ.

Much of what the apostles taught may be traced to the Old Testament revelation given to God's people group national ethnic Israel. Most of what is not from the Old Testament may be traced to what Jesus said in the gospels, e.g., Colossians 2:9.

In other words, much of what the apostles taught it is not new revelation, but preexisting revelation repeated, explained, and applied to a new people group, the New Testament church. Many of Paul's exhortations concerning the believer's behavior have their source in God's revelation through the Old Testament prophets, or Jesus in the gospels.

But there are doctrines, such as the rapture of the New Testament church, that originate through the apostolic witness as received by direct revelation. Therefore, there are times when it is crucial we be reminded of the source of biblical revelation, because those with doubts will distort the doctrine to fit their assumptions. Some deny this doctrine of the rapture of the New Testament church. Paul says it cannot be denied, because it is by revelation from Jesus Christ.

> that we the living remaining unto the coming of the Lord, shall never no never precede those having fallen asleep.

Whenever Christ will return for his New Testament church, there will be living believers to greet him. This, of course, is to be expected. Jesus said, "I will build my church, and the gates of Hades will not prevail against it," Matthew 16:18, that is, will not prevail against the gates to the New Testament church. The city gates were used as a metaphor for strength; gates closed and barred refused entry to the enemy. The city gates were a symbol of permanence, because as long as the gates stood the city was secure. The gates of the New Testament church open only to let new believers enter. They stand unassailable, immune to the power and machinations of Hades.

Excursus: The Gates of Hades

The "gates of *hádēs*," Matthew 16:18, speaks of the power of *hádēs*. Now *hádēs* is a location in the spirit domain where the unsaved dead are imprisoned until the GWT judgment. As such it has no power to threaten the church. So the use here is metaphorical, it stands for something else. The most common and likely interpretation is that "gates of *hádēs*" represents Satan and his fallen angels. The close connection of 16:23, where Jesus said to Peter, "Get behind me Satan," supports the interpretation.

Now, Satan does not rule in *hádēs*, an idea gained from Milton's epic poem *Paradise Lost*. *Hádēs* is for human souls, not fallen angels. Because *hádēs* is the place for lost sinners, and Satan is the originator of sin, through sin Satan may be said to have the power of death, and so by a turn of the figure Satan's strength may be said to be *hádēs*, because that is where all his victims are kept. Satan doesn't really have the power of death; God is the one who gives eternal life and endless punishment.

Because Satan originated sin, and thereby activated God's penalty against sin, which is death, then in a figure Satan as the originator of sin may be said to have the power of death. Moreover, since through temptation to sin Satan brings death to human souls, then he may also be said to have the power of death through his power of temptation. And since the result of an unsaved sinner's death is confinement in *hádēs*, then as the place where his victims are confined the strength of Satan may be said to be the gates of *hádēs*, i.e., his strength is shown in the damnation of his victims.

So this verse is a metaphorical use of the literal place *hádēs*. As such it shows the strength of sin and the strength of death: all unsaved sinners go to *hádēs* from which there is no escape. Sin and death—*hádēs*—shall not prevail against the church, because Jesus is Lord over life and death, and he has given the church eternal life. [Source, Quiggle, *Dispensational Eschatology*, 144–145.]

Returning to the exposition. There will always be a New Testament church. "Father, those you have given me, I desire that where I am they also might be with me," John 17:24. "And so always with the Lord we will be," 1 Thessalonians 4:17. Here we discover that when Christ returns for his church, there will be physically living believers, however long the wait until Christ returns for his church. Those who have predicted, or bewailed, the demise of the New Testament church are in error.

The double negative, "never no never" reflects the Greek text. The Greek language used a double negative to emphasize the impossibility of a thing. There will be a living New Testament church at the rapture, because both physically dead believers and physically living believers will be transformed and glorified at the same event. As Paul will explain, at 4:16, the bodies of the physically dead believers will be resurrected (the physical body recreated without mortality) and reanimated (the person rejoined with his/her body) in a glorified state before the living believers are transformed and glorified. Thus the living do not precede the dead in glorification.

> Resurrection. The reuniting of an individual soul with its original body after physical death has occurred. Resurrection encompasses two processes: 1) God reforms the physically dead body from existing materials and, 2) God causes the disembodied soul originally propagated with that body to unite with it and animate it. The united soul and resurrected body will continue in that reunited state throughout eternity.
>
> In the saved, the death of the body frees the soul from the presence of sin, and the saved soul is immediately transformed and glorified to be eternally incorruptible. Then, when the body of the saved person is resurrected, it is reformed free from the presence of sin and transformed and glorified to be eternally incorruptible. The saved live eternally in the state of reunited body and soul without sin or corruption.
>
> (In the unsaved, resurrection reunites a sinful soul with a sinful

98

and corrupted body to endure judgment and eternal punishment.)

[Source: Quiggle, *Dictionary*]

Both Paul and the Thessalonians believed they personally would be transformed and glorified as living believers and taken to heaven by Jesus Christ. The hope of Christ's return—the rapture—was actively anticipated by the apostolic church. They knew physical death before the rapture was possible, but they daily lived in the assurance of removal from the earth by Christ as living believers. The rapture of the New Testament church is not a new doctrine.

That belief—to be taken to heaven without passing through physical death—raised a question. If Christ was returning for the living New Testament church, what about those believers who had died before he returned? (Notice this indicates some believers had already died in Thessalonica. From persecution?) Paul explains in the next verse.

Translation 1 Thessalonians 4:16

Because the Lord himself, by a loud command, by the voice of an archangel, and by the trumpet of God, will descend from heaven, and the dead in Christ will rise first.

EXPOSITION

"The Lord himself." Jesus Christ will personally, literally, return to take the living church into heaven.

"By a loud command," of whatever nature. Perhaps, like at the tomb of Lazarus, Christ will call the dead to "come forth," and then like John in the Revelation, Christ will call the living church to "come up here." Regardless of the word or words used, the New Testament church will respond to the voice of their Savior.

"By the voice of an archangel." Some believe there is only one archangel, whose name is Michael. He is the only archangel identified by name in Scripture. But he is also identified by his position: he is the one who stands over Israel, Daniel 12:1. The archangel Michael always appears in the context of national ethnic Israel, Daniel 10:13, 21; 12:1; Jude 9; Revelation 12:7. He is the leader of a group of angels assigned by Christ to interface, interact, and protect national ethnic Israel.

The archangel whose voice will be heard at the rapture must be a different archangel, because the New Testament church, not national ethnic Israel, is in view. This archangel is in charge of those angels whose responsibility is to interface, interact, and protect the New Testament church. That he is not named or otherwise identified is not a barrier to his existence. God has more than one people group. There are many people groups in the Son's house, Hebrews 3:2–6. These are: the saved from Adam to Moses; national ethnic Israel; the New Testament church; Tribulation believers; those saved during the millennial kingdom. Perhaps there is an archangel assigned to each group?

What the archangel at the rapture will say is not revealed. We know it is not a command to the New Testament church. Christ commands the church and the angels are his messengers to the church. At a guess, guided by Scripture (e.g., Revelation 5:11–12), he initiates a shout or chant of praise by the angels he commands (angels don't sing, they "say"). The homecoming of the entire New Testament church is an occasion for great praise and glory to Christ.

A trumpet will be sounded. Many try to identify this trumpet as one of the seven to be sounded during the Tribulation, Revelation 8:2. But the consequences of each of those trumpets is explained, and none of those consequences is the gathering of the New Testament church into heaven.

This trumpet will sound in relation to the rapture of the people group, the New Testament church. To discover the identification of this trumpet we must look at the use of a trumpet in relation to another people group. We need look no further than Exodus 13:13 (ESV), "When the trumpet sounds a long blast, they [national ethnic Israel] shall come up to the mountain." The trumpet will call Christ's New Testament church to their assembly with him in the air.

A trumpet is also used to announce the presence of God. Psalm 47:5 (ESV), "God has gone up with a shout, the Lord with the sound of a trumpet." Yes! God has gone up to claim his church from the world, with a loud command and the sound of a trumpet.

In 1 Corinthians 15 Paul names this trumpet the last trumpet.

1 Corinthians 15:52 (ESV), in a moment, in the twinkling of an eye, at the last trumpet. For the trumpet will sound, and the

dead will be raised imperishable, and we shall be changed.

This is the rapture: the dead will be raised, the living shall be changed. This is not the last trumpet to ever sound—we know there are seven during the Tribulation—but it is the last (known) trumpet to sound for the purpose of gathering God's people to himself. Perhaps a trumpet sounds every time a New Testament believer dies and goes to heaven? A last trumpet would sound to gather those remaining.

The Lord Jesus Christ will, "descend out of heaven." Descend to where. Paul says in 4:17 he descends to the air. The air is the atmosphere of the earth. This is not an advent of Christ. An advent of deity is defined as deity with feet on the ground.

> Exodus 3:2–5 (HCSB), Then the Angel of the Lord appeared to him in a flame of fire within a bush. As Moses looked, he saw that the bush was on fire but was not consumed. So Moses thought: I must go over and look at this remarkable sight. Why isn't the bush burning up? When the Lord saw that he had gone over to look, God called out to him from the bush, "Moses, Moses!" "Here I am," he answered." "Do not come closer," He said. "Take your sandals off your feet, for the place where you are standing is holy ground."

> Joshua 5:13–15 (NIV), Now when Joshua was near Jericho, he looked up and saw a man standing in front of him with a drawn sword in his hand. Joshua went up to him and asked, "Are you for us or for our enemies?" "Neither," he replied, "but as commander of the army of the Lord I have now come." Then Joshua fell facedown to the ground in reverence, and asked him, "What message does my Lord have for his servant?" The commander of the Lord's army replied, "Take off your sandals, for the place where you are standing is holy." And Joshua did so.

> Zechariah 14:3–4 (ESV), Then the Lord will go out and fight against those nations as when he fights on a day of battle. On that day his feet shall stand on the Mount of Olives that lies before Jerusalem on the east.

> Luke 2:7, 11–12 (ESV), And she gave birth to her firstborn son and wrapped him in swaddling cloths and laid him in a manger, because there was no place for them in the inn . . . .. "For unto

you is born this day in the city of David a Savior, who is Christ the Lord. And this will be a sign for you: you will find a baby wrapped in swaddling cloths and lying in a manger."

Zechariah 14:4 is of particular importance in this discussion, for it defines the moment of the second advent: Christ's feet on the ground at the Mount of Olives in the Day of the Lord (see Zechariah 14:1).

The return of the Lord Jesus Christ for his New Testament church is not his second advent. He descends to the air, not the ground. The timing is not the Day of the Lord, it is the event that precedes that day, the event that announces its coming. The rapture of the New Testament church is the next scheduled event on God's prophetic calendar, and the scheduled event after that is the Day of the Lord. (I will have more to say about the "air" at 4:17.)

The dead in Christ will rise first. This is the resurrection of the bodies of the physically dead believers of the New Testament church. As previously discussed, Christ will bring with him those New Testament believers who have died prior to his descent to call his church to heaven. He will bring the persons with him as the disembodied souls they became at physical death.

The soul is the person. The physical body is not a prison for the soul (an idea from ancient Greek philosophers). A human being is the union of two dissimilar things: a material body and an immaterial soul, Genesis 2:7. The body cannot be alive without the soul, for it is the soul that contains the animating principle we call "life," again Genesis 2:7.

Christ will bring the persons with him from heaven to the air. Then Christ will command their body be re-created—all will have suffered decomposition, and most will have decomposed into dust and atoms. By his omniscience and omnipotence he will re-create the bodies of the physically dead saved to be immortal and incorruptible, 1 Corinthians 15:52–53. Then he will join the individual souls to their body, thereby animating the body, and that joined state of immortal and incorruptible body and soul will be the condition of the saved endlessly.

The soul of the physically dead believer is already immortal and incorruptible. The Bible never indicates the dissolution of the soul as it does the body. Once the processes of procreation have formed a new soul at conception in the womb, that soul is immortal, it has endless life.

A new soul is conceived with sin. Genesis 5:3 and Romans 5:12 indicate every person inherits the sinful human nature of Adam and Eve. Every mortal human being possesses the sin attribute as part of his or her human nature. Being born-again in salvation does not remove the sin attribute from human nature (but it does remove its dominion, Romans 6:14).

Physical death removes the sin attribute from the human nature of the saved (but not the unsaved). We know this because no sinner stands in God's presence in heaven, and the physically dead believer is "present with the Lord" immediately after physical death. Therefore, those persons Christ brings with him to the rapture are sinless, to be rejoined with their re-created, immortal, incorruptible resurrected body.

Translation 1 Thessalonians 4:17–18

17 Then we the living remaining, together with them, will be caught up in the clouds for the meeting of the Lord in the air. And so always with the Lord we will be. 18 Therefore, encourage one another with these words.

EXPOSITION

The rapture of the New Testament church ("we . . . will be caught up") is first mentioned by Christ, though not by that name, in John 14:2–3.

> In my Father's house are many abiding places; but if not I would have said that to you. I go to prepare a place for you. And when I should go and prepare a place for you, I am coming again and will receive you to myself; that where I am, you may be also.

Paul reveals a definite order to the rapture event. First those whom Christ brings with him are resurrected and reunited with their bodies. Then the entire New Testament church, the resurrected and the living, are called up together to meet the Lord in the air. As the living church is called up, they are transformed and glorified, even as Paul described that event to the Corinthians, "the dead shall be raised incorruptible and we [the living] shall be changed," 1 Corinthians 15:52.

The resurrection of the bodies of the believers Jesus brings with him, and their reunification with their bodies, takes place on the earth, because that is where the bodies lie in wait. "Then," after "the dead in Christ rise," the living church, "together with" the resurrected church, will be "caught up," *hárpazō*, raptured, "in the clouds for the meeting of the Lord in the air."

The use of clouds in this phrase appears to be literal. Clouds are sometimes used to identify the hosts of the Lord of Hosts. For example, Daniel 7:13, the Son of Man is coming "with the clouds of heaven." As heaven is a place in the spirit domain, it seems unlikely it has an atmosphere with literal clouds. This verse in Daniel most likely corresponds in time and place with Revelation 19:14, Christ coming with the armies of heaven. In context, those armies must be angels and the redeemed of the ages.

Clouds in the Thessalonian passage could mean the host of saints the Lord Jesus Christ is bringing with him, 4:14. But the most likely view is literal clouds in the literal atmosphere. That being said, one must consider the meaning of the word translated "air."

The word translated "air" in 4:17 is the Greek word *aḗr* [Zodhiates, s. v. "109"]. The Jews conceived of the *aḗr* as a spirit domain where Satan and his angels lived. The Greeks understood *aḗr* to be a kind of atmosphere that filled the space between the earth and the moon, beyond which was heaven, the abode of higher spirits. Thus, the *aḗr* was the abode of the lower spirits. In biblical use *aḗr* sometimes means earth's atmosphere, e.g., Acts 22:23; Revelation 9:2, and sometimes the spirit domain, e.g., Ephesians 2:2. (All uses: those mentioned plus 1 Corinthians 9:26; 14:9; Revelation 16:17.)

Paul is not conforming to either Jewish or Greek cosmology, but is using and redefining a familiar term to give knowledge and understanding. The meaning of *aḗr* in 1 Thessalonians 4:17 could be earth's atmosphere or the spirit domain. The "clouds" point to the atmosphere. But because the rapture calls the saved to come to the "many abiding places" in "my father's house" (John 14:2), *aḗr* may also be understood as the spirit domain where believers shall live endlessly: heaven.

I believe the meaning is the church is called up into the first heaven, the sky ("clouds"), to meet the Lord in the second heaven, the spirit domain (*aḗr*), to be taken to "my father's house," the third heaven, a location in the spirit domain where God has a permanent manifestation of his presence, Revelation 4.

We know from his second letter that Paul had explained these things in person, 2 Thessalonians 2:15, during his time in Thessalonica Acts 17. The Thessalonian church knew exactly what Paul meant by *aér*. I believe we may view *aér* as first the sky and then the spirit domain.

The rapture event takes the New Testament church to heaven, where the church will always be with the Lord, the fulfillment of Christ's prayer, John 17:24. Paul believed an understanding of the rapture was encouraging. And so it is. Whatever may happen to the believer during this mortal life, he has the guarantee of endless life with Christ, wherever Christ may be. As Paul said in another place, "the sufferings of this present time are not worthy to be compared with the glory which shall be revealed in us" (Romans 8:18). He probably had the rapture in mind when he wrote that verse.

What Paul has said concerning the rapture presents a complete and understandable testimony consistent with John 14:2–3. At an unknown and unknowable date in the future, a date not preceded by any signs to let us know it is coming, Jesus Christ will return to call and receive his church unto himself.

Are there no signs? Many today—and many in the past—have looked for signs of his coming. (Such as Martin Luther, who in AD 1532 saw "signs" and wrote, *The Signs of Christ's Coming and the Last Days*.) Jesus said, "it is not yours to know times or seasons which the Father set by his own authority," Acts 1:7. We cannot know when the rapture will take place. Therefore we should not be looking for so-called "signs of the times" that are supposed to let the church known the rapture is near.

Let us do what the Bible requires: live in the hope of Christ's return. In the Bible "hope" is a steadfast assurance that the thing promised will certainly come to pass. In the world we hope the weather will be good for the picnic: we are anxious about the weather. As Christians we hope Christ will return: we know he will, because Scripture says he will—because he said he will return for his New Testament church. Live in that hope.

We are also to be constantly prepared for the imminent rapture.

John wrote, 1 John 3:3, that "everyone who has this hope [of Christ's return] purifies himself, just as Christ is pure." John didn't mean the hope itself was purifying. He meant that those who have this hope will continue to take action to keep themselves ready—living righteous lives of faith doing righteous works by faith. They will ignore the so-called "signs of the times" and keep themselves ready at all times for the imminent, at-any-moment, return of Jesus Christ for his church at the rapture.

The second passage in 1 Thessalonians that interacts with the rapture is 1 Thessalonians 5:9. The following exegesis is from *A Private Commentary on the Bible: Thessalonians*, beginning on page 154, lightly edited to the present purpose.

Translation 1 Thessalonians 5:9–10a

9 Because God has not appointed us for wrath, but for obtaining deliverance through our Lord Jesus Christ, 10 the one having died for us, so that whether we might watch or we might sleep, we may live together with him.

EXPOSITION

> Because God has not appointed us for wrath, but for obtaining deliverance through our Lord Jesus Christ, the one having died for us.

> The word I have translated "deliverance" is *sōtēría* [Zodhiates, s. v. "4991"]. Most versions translate *sōtēría* in 1 Thessalonians 5:9, as "salvation." The word *sōtēría* means, "safety, deliverance, preservation from danger," not specifically "salvation" in the sense of saved from the penalty due sin. As always context determines the specific meaning.

> In the proper context, e.g., 2 Thessalonians 2:13, *sōtēría* can mean salvation from sins, but not in the context of 1 Thessalonians 5:9. In this verse *sōtēría* is better translated "deliverance," because Paul is writing to people who are already saved. The contrast is between suffering God's wrath and not suffering God's wrath because delivered from God's wrath. A specific application of God's wrath is in view.

> In context, Paul is writing about deliverance from the Tribulation [see 5:2] through the rapture of the New Testament church by Jesus Christ. The better translation is, "Because God has not appointed us for wrath, but for obtaining deliverance through our Lord Jesus Christ." When *sōtēría* is properly translated the meaning is clear, because at no time during its existence does the New Testament church nor any member of the New Testament church experience the wrath of God.

> That is because for the saved person to experience God's wrath would mean Christ's propitiation for sin on the cross did not fully satisfy God for the crime of human sin. Either Jesus Christ paid for every

human sin, past, present, and future, or he did not. (This is not universal salvation, because the merit of that propitiation must be applied to each individual sinner by God's grace through the individual exercise of saving faith. God's grace is applied according to his decree of election, Ephesians 1:4, through the individual application of his gift of grace-faith-salvation, Ephesians 2:8.)

Therefore, the theory the New Testament church will go through the Tribulation denies the completeness of Christ's propitiation for sin for a certain number of believers. The New Testament church is all the people saved from the AD 33 Pentecost to the Rapture. The church physically alive on the cusp of the Tribulation is a tiny portion of the entire New Testament church. Why should that tiny portion be denied the benefits of Christ's propitiation? The answer is, no member of the New Testament church will ever suffer God's wrath.

The answer from the partial rapturists and the post-Tribulation rapturists is the living church at that time are all Laodicean—lukewarm about Christ and therefore must undergo the Tribulation (in part or in whole) to be worthy of going to heaven.

The partial and post-Tribulation rapture views ignore the efficacy of Christ's propitiation of God for all the elect. So also the mid- and pre-wrath rapture views, because they ignore God's wrath begins when the Antichrist begins to exercise his influence on the earth, Daniel 9:27a, which is the beginning of the Tribulation, Revelation 6:2.

The truth of salvation cannot be stated loudly enough or often enough: Jesus Christ endured God's wrath against sin so that not one of his saved people will suffer God's wrath; never no never. The Tribulation is a time of God's wrath upon the earth; the living New Testament church is removed from the earth prior to the Tribulation.

The partial, mid-, pre-wrath, and post- Tribulation rapture views are also ignorant of Scripture: God's wrath is only directed toward those not saved. As pointed out at comments on 5:1–5, the phrase, "those who dwell on the earth," is a Revelation euphemism for the unsaved, 3:10; 6:10; 11:10; 13:8, 14; 14:6; 17:8 (all occurrences).

When the Tribulation begins all on the earth are unsaved, because every believer has been removed from the earth by the rapture. Those saved during the Tribulation do not suffer Gods' wrath on the unsaved, but persevere through the consequences of that wrath. Jesus gave the principle: God sends rain on the just and the unjust (Matthew 5:45).

When the rain causes a flood, the lands of the saved are not miraculously protected from flooding. The believer endures the consequences and recovers (through grace and mercy from God) but God's wrath was not directed at the believer. Noah and family endured the consequences of the world-wide flood, but the wrath of God expressed in the flood fell on the unrighteous. As Peter says (1 Peter 3:20), eight people were saved. The rest were not. So too the Tribulation. Multitudes will be saved as a consequence of God's wrath on the unsaved, Revelation 7:14. The rest will not be saved.

The view that every church—every believer—immediately prior to the Tribulation is a "Laodicean church" kind of believer is unrealistic. The seven churches of Revelation chapters 2 and 3 do not form a prophetic calendar for the New Testament church age. I have a thorough discussion of this view in my commentary on the Revelation 1–7, pages 65–69. The proposed prophetic calendar is:

Ephesus is said to represent the church during the apostolic age, A.D. 33-100.

Smyrna is said to represent the church during the ten persecutions by Rome, A.D. 100-300.

Pergamos is said to represent the union of church and state, A.D. 300-500.

Thyatira is said to represent the period of the Papacy (Holy Roman Catholic church), A.D. 500-1500.

Sardis is said to represent the Reformation period, A.D. 1500-1700.

Philadelphia is said to represent the missionary church, A.D. 1500-1900.

Laodicea is said to represent the worldly, self-satisfied church, 1900-Present.

In brief, the problems with this view are:

It is an historicist view trying to find fulfillment in church history.

The particular order of this "calendar" is a recent development.

Each church will fit into other historical eras, giving a different order.

The "calendar" ignores non-western churches.

The "calendar" ignores the Dissenter churches.

The calendar view assumes the Lord is addressing unbelievers and apostates in the New Testament church, but every New Testament letter, including these seven, are directed at believers. Only believers are able to "repent" and "overcome" (Revelation 2:5, 7, 16, 17, 26; 3:3, 5, 19, 21).

In the calendar view, the greater majority of present-day churches must be Laodicea-type churches, a fact denied by even a casual review of church history from the 1900s forward.

The biblical view is the spiritual state and worldly conditions affecting each of the seven churches can be found everywhere and every-when in New Testament church history, including the present times.

The better interpretation is that these seven churches actually existed and the conditions noted at each church are literal. The conditions noted by Christ reflect genuine problems facing genuine believers; thus they may be found in any local church throughout the history of the church.

The partial, mid-, pre-wrath, and post- Tribulation rapture views fail every test of doctrine and history, because God has not appointed his saved people for wrath, but for obtaining deliverance from that wrath through our Lord Jesus Christ, "the one having died for us."

5:10 . . . so that whether we might watch or we might sleep, we may live together with him.

Here, Paul uses "watch" in the sense of living the Christian life and "sleep" in the figurative sense of physical death. Jesus Christ, having propitiated God for us (having died to satisfy God's justice for our sins) has saved us, so whether physically alive or physically dead we live together with him. The rapture will gather the entire church, "And so always with the Lord we will be."

Revelation 3:10 is another passage that interacts with the rapture. The interpretative value of this passage, in relation to the rapture, is it fixes a time for the rapture in relation to the Day of the Lord, which is more commonly known in these New Testament times as the Tribulation (although it extends to 2 Peter 3:10). This exegesis is from *A Private Commentary on the Bible: Revelation 1–7*, beginning on page 187, lightly edited to the present purpose.

Translation Revelation 3:10

10 Because you have kept the word of my endurance as to circumstances, I also will keep you out of the hour of the trial that is about to come upon the whole inhabited earth, to test the earth dwellers.

TRANSLATION NOTES

The phrase, "endurance as to circumstances" is a more literal translation of the word usually translated "patience" or "endurance." That word is *hupomonḗ* [Zodhiates, s. v. 5281], endurance as to things or circumstances, versus *makrothumía* [Zodhiates, s. v. 3115], endurance with people. God is *makrothumía*, longsuffering with people, never *hupomonḗ*, enduring things or circumstances. The believer is to be both.

At 3:10 a phrase occurs that is used repeatedly in Revelation to identify the unsaved. The phrase is literally, "those dwelling upon the earth." I have consistently given this phrase as "earth dwellers" wherever it occurs in the text of the Revelation.

EXPOSITION

The church at Philadelphia—the people of that local church—had endured the world's opposition to their testimony for Christ. Christ would, in turn, keep them from a specific time of persecution identified as "the trial that is about to come upon the whole inhabited earth, to test the earth-dwellers."

The first thing to notice is the purpose of this trial: not to test believers, but the unsaved, identified here as "the earth dwellers." The phrase "earth dwellers" occurs nine times in the Revelation, 3:10; 6:0;

11:10; 13:8; 14:14; 14:6; 17:8. Each time it specifically refers to the unsaved.

Revelation 3:10, Because you have kept the word of my endurance as to circumstances, I also will keep you out of the hour of the trial that is about to come upon the whole inhabited earth, to test the earth dwellers.

Revelation 6:10, And they were exclaiming in a loud voice, saying, "Until when, O Lord, holy and true, do you not judge and avenge our blood from those dwelling upon the earth?"

Revelation 11:10, And the earth dwellers are glad over them and rejoice, and will send gifts to one another, because these two prophets did afflict the earth dwellers.

Revelation 13:8, And all earth dwellers will worship it, of whom their names have not been written in the book of life of the Lamb, the one that was slain from the founding of the world.

Revelation 13:14, And it deceives the earth dwellers by means of the signs that were given to it to do in the presence of the beast, telling those earth dwellers to make an image to the beast that has the sword wound and has lived.

Revelation 14:6, And I saw another messenger, flying in mid-heaven, having the everlasting good news to proclaim upon the earth dwellers, and upon every nation, and tribe, and language, and people.

Revelation 17:8, "The beast, the one you saw, was, and is not, and is about to ascend out of the abyss, and go into damnation. And the earth dwellers will wonder, those whose names are not written in the book of life from the foundation of the world, seeing the beast that was, and is not, and yet will be.

Jesus at Revelation 3:10 is not promising no further trials or persecution for the Philadelphia church. He is predicting a time of worldwide trial for the unsaved, a period of time in which the church will not participate.

No such worldwide trial of all the unsaved in the world has occurred from AD 96 to the present date of AD 2022. The prediction was and is for a yet-future time.

Therefore, what Jesus has to say about this time of worldwide trial is not just for the local church at Philadelphia in AD 96. The scope of the trial is worldwide, therefore the exclusion from the trial must also be worldwide. The time of the trial is historically proven to be yet-future—it hasn't happened yet—therefore Jesus must be speaking all the yet-future churches. Jesus is using the church at Philadelphia to tell his churches worldwide, at a yet-future time, that he will keep his saved people "out of" the worldwide trial that will come upon every unsaved person in the world, upon the earth dwellers.

"The hour of the trial" is a figure of speech that does not refer to duration, but to an event occurring at a time yet-future to the time Jesus gave the prediction. The date of the event is predetermined: the hour of the trial is a specific trial occurring at a specific time in history. The date in history was yet-future when the prediction was given, and the history of the world that has already passed reveals the event is still yet-future.

The purpose of this particular hour of trial is to determine the true character of those being tested. The issue to be tested concerns one's relationship to God in Christ: faith in or rejection of Christ. The matter of testing has been established in 3:8–9: to keep Jesus' commandments and name. In the context of, "the earth dwellers," the test is to positively respond to the commandment to believe on God and God's testimony of the coming Messiah-Redeemer-King, Jesus the Christ.

The New Testament church will be kept "out of" the coming hour of trial. This cannot refer to the usual trials and persecutions of the church. John 16:33, Jesus said to his disciples, "in the world you have affliction. But be courageous, I have overcome the world." Jesus cannot be contradicting himself at Revelation 3:10.

The word translated "out of" in Revelation 3:10 is *ek* [Zodhiates, s. v. 1537], a preposition meaning out of, from. In none of the 928 occurrences in the New Testament does *ek* mean "during." Wallace [371] says when *ek* is used in the sense of separation it has the force of "away from, from." In Revelation 3:10 the sense is separation: the church is to be separated from the hour of trial.

The "hour of trial" is that specific event known as the Tribulation period of time. We know this from the repeated use of "earth dwellers" in 3:10 and throughout the Revelation. That hour of trial—the Tribulation—is the subject of the eschatological passages in Matthew,

Mark, and Luke, and the word (*thlípsis*) is specifically mentioned at Matthew 24:21, 29; Mark 13:19, 24. In the Revelation the word, *thlípsis* [Zodhiates, s. v. 2347] is used in the sense of the 3:10 hour of trial only at 7:14. The other fifteen uses of *thlípsis* generally speak of the affliction Christians experience in the world.

Bottom line: Jesus says no New Testament church will experience the yet-future hour of trial more commonly known as the Tribulation. The purpose of the trial is for the unsaved; the preposition *ek* means out of the hour of trial, not during the hour of the trial.

The passage in 2 Thessalonians 2:1–3 interacts with the timing of the rapture. Below is an exegesis of the passage from *A Private Commentary on the Bible: Thessalonians*, beginning on page 205, lightly edited to the present purpose.

Translation 2 Thessalonians 2:1–2

1 Now we implore you, brothers, by the coming of our Lord Jesus Christ and our gathering together unto him, 2 for you to not quickly be wavering in mind nor be disturbed, neither by spirit nor by word nor by letter, as if by us, as though the Day of the Lord is present.

EXPOSITION

Paul now turns to his primary reason for writing this letter. Someone was teaching the Day of the Lord was present. That teaching contradicted what Paul had taught them during his time in Thessalonica, and what he had written in his first letter.

The Day of the Lord is the Tribulation period following the "last time-last hour," which is the entire New Testament church dispensation, 1 John 2:18; 1 Peter 1:5; Jude 18. When the "last time-last hour," has ended, the Day of the Lord begins. All are unsaved at the beginning of the Day of the Lord. During the Day of the Lord, God moves in judgment and salvation preparatory to the second advent and the Davidic-Messianic-Millennial Kingdom.

Scripture discussions of the Day of the Lord usually incorporate the second advent. However, 2 Peter 3:10–13 looks to the end of the current heavens and earth, Revelation 20:11; 21:1, not the Tribulation or advent. Other scriptures: Isaiah 2:12; 13:6, 9; Ezekiel 30:3; Joel 3:14; Obadiah 15; Zephaniah 1:7, 8, 14, 18; Malachi 4:5; Acts 2:20; 1 Thessalonians 5:2; 2 Peter 3:10.

Sometimes is it referred to as "that day," e.g., Isaiah 19; 52:6; Ezekiel 38:19; Zechariah 14:9. Once it is referred to as "the time of Jacob's trouble," Jeremiah 30:7. (See my work, *Dispensational Eschatology* for a thorough discussion of Day of the Lord and related terms.)

Someone pretending to be the apostle Paul, by a letter supposedly from Paul, or pretending to communicate a new prophesy concerning the future (by spirit), or pretending to communicate a teaching from Paul (by word) had told the Thessalonian believers the persecutions and tribulations they had been experiencing were because the Day of the Lord had arrived. Paul says that teaching was false; he said, "as though" it was present, indicating it was not present.

We know Paul had taught them about the Day of the Lord, 2:2, that period of time the New Testament names the Tribulation. We know Paul also taught a man of lawlessness would come after the rapture, 2:1–3, 5. The context implies a certain order: the coming of Christ to gather his New Testament church out of the world, the Day of the Lord in the world, the man of lawlessness during the Day of the Lord.

In the commentary on First Thessalonians I explained the difference between Christ's coming to the air for the New Testament church before the Tribulation, which is the rapture, and his coming to the earth at the end of the Tribulation, which is the second advent. The return to the air for the New Testament church is not an advent. Zechariah 14:4 and Luke 2:7 define an advent of deity: deity with feet on the ground. First the rapture, then the Day of the Lord, the man of lawlessness during the Day of the Lord, then the second advent of Jesus Christ.

Paul wrote in 2 Thessalonians 1 to set their present persecutions and tribulations within an eschatological context. Christ was coming, "to inflict vengeance on those not knowing God and on those not obeying the gospel of our Lord Jesus," his second advent. Their current suffering at the hands of the world was a testimony of that yet-future second coming to inflict vengeance; after the advent would be the kingdom, 1:5. And in that sense, their persecutions and tribulations were laying up treasure in the present for the glory they would bring to Christ at his coming, 1:10.

What these Thessalonians were experiencing in this present world was and is normal to the Christian life, and to be expected, as prior to "the coming of our Lord Jesus Christ and our gathering together unto him, " and prior to "the Day of the Lord." Our "gathering together with him" is the rapture, 1 Thessalonians 4:13–18. The word "gathering" is not used in that passage, but the fact of our gathering at his coming is present: "Then we the living remaining, together with them [the resurrected], will be caught up in the clouds for the meeting of the Lord in the air."

Paul said, 2:1, I appeal to the fact of our gathering at the coming of Christ prior to the Day of the Lord, that you be not wavering or disturbed as though the Day of the Lord is present; as though your persecutions and tribulations were because the Tribulation was present. The phrase, "by the coming of," indicates the coming of Christ to gather the New Testament church had not yet come but was yet-future. Therefore the Tribulation (the Day of the Lord) had not yet come. Paul specifically denies having told them in any possible manner that the Tribulation had come.

The affirmation that Christ had not yet come to gather his New Testament church, and the denial the Day of the Lord was present, must guide our views of the relevant eschatological events. Christ comes and gathers the New Testament church prior to the Tribulation period. Therefore, any kind of persecutions and tribulations experienced prior to the coming of Christ to gather his church are normal to the times of the New Testament church, which extend from the AD 33 Pentecost to the yet-future rapture of the New Testament church, 1 John 2:18; 1 Peter 1:5; Jude 18.

Translation 2 Thessalonians 2:3

3 No one should deceive you in any way, because not until the departure shall have come first, and the man of lawlessness shall have been revealed, the son of destruction

EXPOSITION

Now follows a long discussion of the words, "the departure."

There is an ellipsis in 2:3 that must be supplied by inserting a phrase from 2:2. In 2:2 Paul refers to some teaching the Thessalonians had received which pretended to be from Paul that, "the Day of the Lord is present." Paul's response in 2:3 refers to that phrase without repeating it. Filling in the ellipsis:

> 2:3 No one should deceive you in any way, because [the Day of the Lord is] not [present] until the departure shall have come first.

The Day of the Lord and the revealing of the man of lawlessness come after "the departure."

The identification of "the departure" has been the subject of keen and vigorous debate in Christianity. I will not resolve that issue here for those convinced otherwise, but I will present what I believe is Paul's meaning.

In context, the "departure" must be "our gathering together unto him," which is to say, the rapture of the New Testament church.

There are two subjects presented in 2:1–2.

the coming of our Lord Jesus Christ and our gathering together unto him

the Day of the Lord

If, as is required by the Literal hermeneutic, we develop our interpretation from context, then the context is, "the Day of the Lord is not present because our gathering together unto him has not yet occurred."

I have previously shown the specific phrase, "our gathering together unto him," indicates the *hárpazō*, the "snatching away" or "caught up," 1 Thessalonians 4:17, is the rapture of the New Testament church. Paul tells the Thessalonians that "the Day of the Lord will be present" after the rapture of the New Testament church, "our gathering together unto him," has occurred.

If we expand the context to what comes after 2:1–3, there is nothing that suggests "the departure" is anything other than what the immediate context suggests: the rapture of the New Testament church. [Not in this book but in the commentary I explain "the one restraining" in its proper place.]

If we expand the context to chapter 1, there is nothing in chapter 1 that suggests "the departure" is anything other than the rapture of the New Testament church. If we expand the context to Paul's first Thessalonian letter, there is nothing in that letter that suggests "the departure" is anything other than the rapture of the New Testament church.

From whence then, different interpretations? The common interpretation is not "the departure" but either the apostasy of the New Testament church, or apostasy in the world. Those interpretations are not from the immediate context of Paul's two Thessalonians letters but are based on church history, beginning with Justin Martyr, and the transliteration, not the translation, of the Greek word *apostasía*.

The word I have translated "the departure" is *apostasía* [Zodhiates, s. v. "646"]. The word means "departure." The word *apostasía* is the feminine form of the noun *aphístēmi* [Zodhiates, s. v. "868"], which means "to depart." But you would not know *apostasía* meant "departure" by looking at the various Bible versions.

— Douay-Rheims, for unless there come a revolt first

— KJV, except there come a falling away first

— YLT, if the falling away may not come first

— ASV, except the falling away come first

— Darby, because [it will not be] unless the apostasy have first

— NIV, until the rebellion occurs

— NKJV, unless the falling away comes first

— NASB, unless the apostasy comes first

— HSCB/CSB, unless the apostasy comes first

— ESV, unless the rebellion comes first

— NRSV, unless the rebellion comes first

— NLT, until there is a great rebellion against God

— Bible Basic English, because there will first be a falling away from the faith

— Easy to Read, the turning away from God

— Jerusalem Bible, the great revolt has taken place

— Phillips NT, a definite rejection of God

— Barclay, the Great Rebellion

In the face of so much evidence to the contrary, how can I justify translating *apostasía* as "the departure" with the interpretation Paul uses this word to indicate the rapture of the New Testament church?

Here is why. All the above translations, beginning with the AD 1582 Douay-Rheims NT (which is an English translation of the 4th century Vulgate), are based on one simple fact: the transliteration of *apostasía* as "apostasy." Not the translation of *apostasía*, but transliteration: the exchange of a Greek alphabet character with the equivalent English alphabet character. The word "apostasy" has the religious sense of departure from true doctrine. That religious sense has affected the various interpretive "translations" of *apostasía*.

The word *apostasía* has a history in secular Greek to indicate political rebellion. The LXX also uses the word to indicate political rebellion, as well as religious rebellion. Some expositors believer Paul has adopted a Jewish tradition, "which speaks of complete apostasy from God and his Torah shortly before the appearance of the Messiah" [Kittel, 1:513]. At Acts 21:21, Paul is accused of *apostasía* from the Torah. There the word is properly translated as "forsake."

The application of a religious sense in 2 Thessalonians 2:3 may, perhaps, be traced back to Justin Martyr (AD 100–165). In his *Dialogue with Trypho* [chapter 110)], what Justin wrote has been translated as, "He [Jesus Christ], shall come from heaven with glory, when the man of apostasy . . . shall venture to do unlawful deeds" [Roberts, *ANF*, 1:253]. The translator of Justin's writings made the choice to transliterate *apostasía*.

Justin, and those following after him, for centuries, have interpretively chosen to associate *apostasía* with "the man of lawlessness" rather than "our gathering together unto him."

As I noted in the beginning of this section, Paul told the Thessalonians the man of lawlessness comes *after* the departure. He himself is not the departure. Whether we interpret *apostasía* as the rapture of the New Testament church or as a departure from right doctrine, the man of lawlessness comes after the *apostasía*. He is not the man of *apostasía*, he is the man of *anomía* [Zodhiates, s. v. "458"], the violation of God's Law.

Some, realizing that particular sequence of events (the *apostasía*, then the man of lawlessness), have departed slightly from Justin's view that the *apostasía* is the man of lawlessness. Instead, their view is the New Testament church commits religious departure from right doctrine. Without a shred of evidence within the context of the Thessalonian letters, or Paul's writings, or the rest of the New Testament, based solely on the history of secular use of *apostasía* and Acts 21:21 (its only other occurrence), these interpreters say the New Testament church will experience a general apostasy from the faith prior to the Day of the Lord and the coming of man of lawlessness.

Just how likely is that scenario? Another long discussion is required, because there is much confusion on this issue.

Looking at the context of the two letters to the Thessalonian church, that scenario is highly unlikely. Paul never mentions to the Thessalonian believers there will be some kind of religious departure from the faith, unless it is 2:3.

Did Paul teach them about a religious departure during his time in Thessalonica? That is speculation unsupported by Scripture, unless 2:3 is that notice. But 2:3 is better explained by what we know Paul did teach: the rapture, then the Day of the Lord and the man of lawlessness.

Let us remind ourselves that the faith some say the New Testament church will depart from is the faith the Thessalonians (and all genuine believers) are constantly proclaiming; the faith for which believers are constantly suffering; the faith Paul says will glorify Christ at his coming. There is nary a hint in either letter that any Thessalonian believer, individually or the Thessalonian church corporately, were experiencing a departure from the faith.

So, why does this idea of a general departure from the faith persist in Bible versions and commentaries? Because it is imported from other New Testament scriptures through a misunderstanding of what the New Testament scriptures teach about the age of the New Testament church.

First, what is the nature of the New Testament church age. The entire New Testament church age, from the AD 33 Pentecost to the yet-future rapture, is the last time-last hour before the end times. 1 John 2:18; 1 Peter 1:5; Jude 18. When Paul, and John, and Jude, and Peter speak of false doctrine and immoral behavior growing worse in the last time they are speaking of false religion and immoral conditions affecting the entire New Testament church age. Paul's equivalent term is "last days," e.g., 2 Timothy 3:1.

Will false religions and immoral behavior become worse as the New Testament church age progresses. Yes, of course. What is characteristic of the entire age will grow worse as the age progresses, because it is the character of the world—not the church—to reject God.

A simple historical example. The New Testament church that slowly developed into the Roman Catholic Church began scripturally, but more and more departed from right doctrine and right behavior over the course of 1,000 years (ca. AD 590 to the Reformation), until true faith was almost lost to the world. Religious and worldly conditions were so bad the Reformer Martin Luther thought the second coming was about to occur, writing and publishing his book in AD 1532, "*The Signs of Christ's Coming and the Last Days.*" But the rapture of the New Testament church did not come.

Another historical example. The Reformation instituted religious and moral reforms that affected the world for the good. But has the world become more religiously and morally false over the course of past 500 years (AD 1517–2022)? Yes, the world has become more religiously and morally false. But the rapture still has not come, even though many calculated the day of the rapture, e.g., in 1843 (Millerite movement) and many today believe the rapture and tribulation are near. (The rapture is always imminent, never near.)

So scriptures in Paul and Peter and Jude that seem to predict a departure from the faith as the immediate precursor of the Day of the Lord, are actually describing conditions repeatedly recurring throughout the New Testament church age, and growing worse—not growing worse in the genuine body of Christ, but in the world. In no Scripture is the amount or quality of "worse" so defined as to allow a prediction of the nearness of the rapture or Tribulation.

Widening our view, Europe, America, and China are currently experiencing a religious and moral decline, but other parts of the world are experiencing a religious and moral revival. The history of the church and the world do not teach a general religious departure by the New Testament church prior to the coming of the Day of the Lord and the man of lawlessness.

Let us turn our attention to Christ's letters to seven churches, Revelation 2, 3, which are often used to say the rapture and Tribulation are near. In those letters we see a departure from the faith and immorality within some of the New Testament churches. But do those letters predict a general departure from the faith in the New Testament church as the precursor to the Day of the Lord?

No. Christ is writing to believers, and some of those churches do have significant problems. But, and this is highly important, they are still his churches, and they are still his people. He calls them to repent;

he invites them to fellowship. Equally as important, there is no contextual connection between the conditions at any one church to the coming Day of the Lord.

Some believe the order of the letters and the conditions at each church present a "prophetic calendar" of the New Testament age, leading up to a general apostasy in the church immediately prior to the Day of the Lord that is characterized by the conditions at the Laodicean church. I have previously addressed that supposed chronology in this book in the chapter "First Thessalonians 5:9." There is no such chronology. See also my book *A Private Commentary on the Bible: Revelation 1–7*, 65–69.

How likely it is Paul was teaching the Thessalonians in 2:3 that there will be a general apostasy of the New Testament church from the faith prior to the Day of the Lord and the coming of man of lawlessness? Highly unlikely.

> The New Testament church belonging to Jesus Christ will never depart from the faith.

> The church the world sees is always departing from the faith.

> Religious apostasy and immorality are the characteristics of the world during the entire New Testament church age.

The immediate context for 2:3 supports the interpretation that "the departure" is "our gathering together unto him," 2:1. Nothing in the rest of the New Testament detracts from that interpretation.

> 2:3 No one should deceive you in any way, because [the Day of the Lord is] not [present] until the departure shall have come first, and the man of lawlessness shall have been revealed, the son of destruction.

The Day of the Lord is present after the rapture when the man of lawlessness is revealed.

Can We Know When?

Should Christians be looking for signs of the times? The Bible and Church history, recent and ancient, compels one to answer this question "No." But today many Christians are looking for signs, whatever these might be, in an attempt to determine if the rapture and Tribulation are "near." I placed that word "near" in quotes to highlight it because it is important to understand that the quest for nearness is not the same as faith in Christ's imminent return. The rapture is imminent: likely to occur at any moment. If, as is the case, there are no signs for the rapture that ends the church age, and if, as is the case, the Tribulation follows the church age, then logically there can be no signs occurring during the church age that would herald the nearness of the Tribulation or the rapture. Signs for the nearness of the Tribulation would be signs for the rapture. But the rapture is imminent. The rapture has been likely to occur at any moment since Christ's ascension in AD 33.

The Biblical Answer: We Cannot Know

There are no signs either the rapture of the Tribulation is near. Jesus said believers cannot know when the Tribulation will occur, Acts 1:7. That is, he said believers cannot know when Messiah will restore the Davidic kingdom, which is immediately after the second advent. Since the second advent is at the end of the Tribulation, to know the timing of one is to know the beginning of the other; to know when the Tribulation will begin is to know the timing of the rapture. Jesus said we cannot know. We should believe him.

The rapture has been imminent since Christ ascended. In Acts 1:11, two angels said to the disciples, "This Jesus, having been taken up from you into heaven, will thus come even as you saw him going into heaven." The angels' statement must have been both encouraging and disappointing: encouraging because Jesus was coming again; disappointing because Jesus had just told them, 1:7, they could not know when he was returning: he said no one could know. One assumes the Tribulation follows shortly after the rapture. "Shortly" is perhaps the wrong term. In prophecy, terms such as "shortly, quickly, suddenly" e.g., Revelation 1:1, do not mean the event is near, or soon to occur, but that when the event does occur it will be conducted quickly, and will swiftly come to its appointed conclusion. To say the Tribulation will begin "shortly" after the rapture is to say it may be days, weeks, months, years, decades after the rapture.

If there are signs that can be interpreted to divulge the nearness of either the rapture or the Tribulation, then by knowing one, the nearness of the other can be known. For this reason many earnestly seek for signs that might point to the nearness of the rapture or Tribulation. The faith, then, of many, is not hope in an imminent rapture—hope in the biblical sense of certainty—but an anxious quest for, "Signs that can tell us if the Tribulation is near; or the rapture." The biblical answer is, "We cannot know," but the quest continues.

It is logically and biblically impossible that there should be signs for the rapture. If there were a sign, then the rapture would be near, not imminent. Since it could happen at any moment, then there can be no signs announcing when "any moment" has arrived. The "sign" that the rapture is "near" is its occurrence. That is because the rapture could occur at any moment; it is imminent.

How do we know the rapture is imminent? Because the Bible does not give any signs predicting its nearness. We have looked at everything Paul said concerning the rapture, and below what Jesus said. Neither Jesus nor Paul gave a date, time, or signs. Paul said the rapture would come with a command, a voice, a trumpet. He did not give any advance signs that would advise the believer when these were about to occur.

Not all would agree with this analysis, because many are looking for the rapture midway through the Tribulation, and others at the end of the Tribulation. If the rapture is midway or at the end, it is not imminent: it is a known date on the prophetic calendar, either at the Abomination of Desolation, or 1,260 days after that event. Is the rapture before, midway, or at the end of the Tribulation? Forests have been felled to make paper for that discussion; I am probably not going to resolve the issue here for the mid-, pre-wrath, partial, and post-tribulation positions. However, I think Jesus and Paul did a good job of telling us that the timing of the rapture and Tribulation cannot be known; i.e., we cannot know when either is "near." Paul specifically told the Thessalonians (second letter) to stop looking at current events because the signs of the Tribulation would occur after the rapture. No one can know if or when the rapture or the Tribulation is near, nor know a date or time as to when one or the other will occur. Jesus specifically said we cannot know in Matthew 24:23, 36–39, 42–44, and Acts 1:7.

Revelation's Answer: We Cannot Know

Some people think Revelation 4:1, the call to John to "come up here," symbolizes the rapture. Whether it does or not is another discussion. If the call to John is to be used as a metaphor of the rapture, let us note there are no signs or dates.

Some people believe the order of the churches in Revelation 2, 3 is a prophetic time-line leading to the Tribulation, and it is so obvious to those people that the church is living in the last days or last times before the Tribulation; therefore, the rapture must be near. But the entire church age, from Christ's resurrection to the rapture, is the last times—not the end-times, but the last times before the end-times, 1 Peter 1:20; 1 John 2:18; Jude 18. (I briefly discussed this supposed prophetic timeline in the chapter "First Thessalonians 5:9. See also *A Private Commentary on the Bible, Revelation 1–7*, 65–69.)

Jesus' Answer: We Cannot Know

The following scriptures tell the church dispensation believer to be watching for Jesus himself, not for signs that might herald his coming. The believer is to be prepared for the rapture by continuously living a righteous life with righteous works. See Philippians 3:20, 21 and compare with 1 Corinthians 15:51–52. The whole of Philippians 3 speaks to being prepared. See Colossians 3:4 and notice the "therefore" at 3:5, indicating one is to do the things from 3:5 through 4:6 in order to be prepared. First Timothy 6:11–15 and Titus 2:11–14 preach the same exhortation. James 5:8 warns believers to be patient, and live a righteous life, because the coming of the Lord is "at hand." The phrase "at hand" does not mean soon or near but means the appearance of the Lord is the next event on God's prophetic calendar. First John 3:2, 3 references the rapture and speaks of being ready.

At Revelation 3:3 Jesus tells the spiritually dead church, Sardis, to hold fast, repent, and watch. What were they to watch for? The things they had received and heard, same verse, which looks back to v. 2, "be watchful and strengthen the things which remain." The believers at

Sardis—believers with a worldly reputation and spiritual deadness (any church at any time during the church age) were not to watch for signs, but to be watchful over their Christian practice, lest they be unprepared for Jesus' coming for the church. The New Testament writers never connected the rapture with watching for signs, but exhorted believers to be prepared at all times for Christ's at-any-moment coming.

Jesus' Olivet discourse in Matthew 24, Mark 13, and Luke 21 begins with the destruction of the temple ("When will these things be," i.e., when will not one stone be left upon another in the temple). It then skips the church age—because it is not important to the Davidic-Messianic Kingdom—and speaks to the Tribulation period. Note that Jesus didn't give an answer of signs or dates that would indicate when the Tribulation was near, but specifically said no one could name the date when the Tribulation would begin. The signs Jesus gave were to help national ethnic Israelis know when they were in the Tribulation and were to start looking for Jesus to return and rescue them. As noted before, the eschatology of the New Testament church dispensation—which includes the rapture of the church—is not in the Synoptic Gospels.

In general terms (Jesus doesn't get specific; that is what the book of Revelation is for), the events he described in (all references Matthew 24) vv. 7–13 reflect the events of the first five seals of Revelation 6. Verse 14 reflects Revelation 14:6–7. Verse 15 is the mid-point of the tribulation, the "middle of the seven" of Daniel 9:27. Verse 20 reflects Revelation 12:13–17. Verses 21–22 are the latter 1,260 days. Verses 23–28 are the Antichrist-beast and false prophet deceiving the world. Verse 27 looks to Revelation 11:15–19; 16:17. Verse 28 corresponds to Revelation 14:17–20. Verses 29–30 correspond to the sixth seal and the seventh bowl, Revelation 6:12–17; 16:18–21. Verse 30 corresponds to Revelation 14:14–16.

In other words, Jesus answered the disciple's first question by saying, "When you see these events happening, that is when these things will be." He answered question two by saying, "My coming will be as unmistakable as the lightning." The answer to question three was, "When my sign appears in heaven it marks the end of the age," i.e., the end of the Tribulation and beginning of the Davidic Kingdom.

In the parable of Matthew 24:32–35 Jesus is again answering their questions in general terms: when you see these things happening—events occurring during the Tribulation—then my coming and the end of the age is near. Verses 36–39 state no one can know the timing or know when these things are near. Verses 40–41 speak of unbelievers in Israel taken away in judgment and believers in Israel left behind to enter the Kingdom. Verses 42–44 again state no one can know when the Tribulation is near. These are not scriptures for the New Testament church. As stated in an earlier chapter. Jewish men are asking the Jewish Messiah about the Jewish Davidic-Messianic Kingdom of 2 Samuel 7:13, 16; Psalm 2.

Five times Jesus said no one can know.

> Matthew 24:23, Jesus said, "Then if anyone says to you, 'Look, here is the Christ,' or 'Here,' do not believe.."

No one can know when Christ will return. If they say they know, "Do not believe it."

> Matthew 24:36, Jesus said, "But about that day and hour no one knows, not even the messengers of the heavens, nor the Son, except Father only."

No one can know when the tribulation begins or when Christ will return.

> Matthew 24:37–39, Jesus said, "For as were the times of Noah, so will be the coming of the Son of Man. For as they were in those times, before the flood, eating and drinking, marrying and giving in marriage, until that day Noah entered into the ark, and they knew not until the flood came and took all away; and so will the coming of the Son of Man."

Jesus used the Noahic Flood as an example. Most people reading the passage miss the point. Here is the point: No one, not Noah, not anyone, only God, knew when the flood would begin. The sign for the flood was "Get in the ark, now," Genesis 7:1. So, too, the sign for the rapture is the rapture; the sign for the Tribulation is Daniel 9:27a. No other signs given.

> Matthew 24:42–44, Jesus said, "Therefore keep watch, because you do not know on what day your Lord is coming. But know this, that if the householder had known in what watch of the night the thief comes, he would have watched, and not have

allowed his house to be broken into. And on account of this, you be ready, for the Son of Man comes in that hour you do not expect."

Verses 42–44 are a warning of judgment directed to unbelievers. Jesus is saying: I have told you before it happens; don't be unbelieving; know and believe and be saved. Jesus point is don't look for signs: believe today and be saved.

Acts 1:6, "Indeed, therefore, those gathered together were asking him, saying, "Lord, if at this time, are you restoring the kingdom to Israel?" The apostles asked Jesus if he would "at this time restore the kingdom."

The apostles were referencing the Davidic-Messianic Kingdom promised to David's heir, 2 Samuel 7:12–13. This is the kingdom promised to God's Anointed—his Messiah-Christ—at Psalm 2. Jesus responded to their question at Acts 1:7. "He said to them, "It is not yours to know the times or seasons which the Father has placed in his own authority." Jesus knew, but he clearly and unequivocally stated that no one else could know. Not holy angels, not fallen angels, not human beings. If there were signs, then we would know. But only God knows.

How much plainer does Jesus need to be? There are no signs to tell us when the rapture or tribulation is near. Jesus said, "Don't Look For Signs," and "You Cannot Know When." Why, then, are you still seeking a sign?

At no time in the discourse did Jesus give a sign occurring before the Tribulation, a sign that the Jews, or anyone else, could use to determine if the Tribulation was near. (The same is true if we like Mark 13 or Luke 21 better than Matthew.)

Stop looking for signs of the times. The only sign the New Testament church was given is the assurance Jesus is coming again, John 14:3. Live every day as though Today was The Day, 1 John 3:1–3.

Objections To The Doctrine Answered

But I hear an objection: Matthew 24:5–13 could apply to conditions before the Tribulation. That is the problem; they apply to almost any year, practically every year, between Christ's ascension and second advent. The signs in the discourse are there to tell the Jews when *they* are in the Tribulation. Do we see similar signs during the church dispensation? Yes, of course, because the church dispensation is the last time before the end times, i.e., the New Testament church dispensation must end before the Tribulation begins. Therefore, every spiritual and moral and ethical condition required to set the specific circumstances necessary for the Tribulation period has always existed during the entire period of the church dispensation, because the rapture is always imminent, never near, and the Tribulation follows the rapture. That is to say, since the rapture is always imminent, and the Tribulation to follow the rapture, then the circumstances of the world are at all times in readiness for the rapture and Tribulation.

This is what frustrates believers looking for signs, and tries Satan's patience. Since the rapture could have occurred at any moment since Christ ascended, Satan has kept the world in constant preparedness for the Tribulation. Why? Because he doesn't know when the rapture and Tribulation will occur. For almost 2,000 years Satan has manipulated the religions, politics, economics, etc., of the world so that, should the rapture occur, he and the world would be ready for the Tribulation. Satan has brought man after man into a position that, should the rapture occur, he would be prepared with a would-be biblical-world-ruler for the Tribulation. Satan is doing better than many believers—to their shame!—in that he is constantly waiting, watching, and prepared for the rapture (as believers are supposed to be) so he can press forward into the Tribulation with an anti-Christian world prepared for his anti-Christian man.

The church doesn't need and shouldn't be looking for someone to tell the times, signs, and seasons, because every Christian since Christ ascended has been living in the times, signs, and seasons preceding the rapture and Tribulation. Do I need to be more plain? The church dispensation is itself the sign that the rapture always was, is now, and always will be (until it happens), imminent; likely to occur at any moment. Every moment of the church dispensation is the sign that the church dispensation is the last times before the end-times begins, 1 Peter 1:20; 1 John 2:18; Jude 18. Therefore, there are no specific signs to tell us when the rapture or Tribulation might be near, because every so-called sign only indicates what is already known: the rapture is imminent, the Tribulation to follow.

The sign-seekers say, "The Tribulation is closer now than it has ever been. That must mean it is near." That is precisely what Martin Luther thought in AD 1532 when he wrote, *The Signs of Christ's Coming and the Last Days*. "But" the sign-seekers say, "there are wars, the threat of world-wide famine, just like Revelation says." Yes, many wars and many famines in the many years from the first century leading to today, none of which resulted in the rapture or Tribulation. A view based upon worldly circumstances will always fail, because there are no signs and no one can know.

"But" I hear again, "by golly Israel is in the land! Surely that means the Tribulation is near." No, it doesn't. Israel in the land since AD 1948 is not a fulfillment of prophecies, such as Jeremiah 23:3–8, because 1) all the Jews aren't in the land; 2) Christ hasn't sent his angels to gather all the Jews out of the rest of the world into the land.

Is Israel in the land a sign the Tribulation is near? Some misunderstand the word "generation" in Matthew 24:34 and misapply it to Israel today. The length of a generation is hotly debated as 20, 25, 25–35, 50, or even 100 years. This view says that because Israel returned to the land in AD 1948, the Tribulation must occur before that 1948 generation passes away. Well, it has been sixty-five years (in 2013) and the rapture and Tribulation haven't happened yet.

The term "generation" in the context of Matthew 24:34 does not mean when the Tribulation begins, but how long it lasts, and more importantly, its effect on the faithful of that generation living when it occurs. In that context, "pass away" takes on new meaning. The generation living at the time the Tribulation begins will not completely die out (cf. vv. 21, 22) before the Tribulation concludes. In other words, some of the faithful will survive to enter the kingdom.

Let me propose a biblically based scenario, using current historical circumstances. Suppose next month Israel's enemies rally sufficient signatures to force a United Nations (UN) resolution revoking the charter that created the Israeli nation? The UN created Israel; therefore they can dissolve the nation. Now what? If the nation of Israel suddenly ceased to exist, is the Tribulation not near? For that matter, how can the Tribulation occur if Israel is not in the land? The answer to this imagined scenario would be Daniel 9:27. Under the terms of this imaginative scenario the Antichrist could make a covenant with many that would restore the Jews to a newly created nation of Israel.

So, Israel in the land today is not a sign that the Tribulation is near; it is merely a current historical circumstance; one of many that have occurred during the past (almost) 2,000 years. Only when the covenant of Daniel 9:27 is made, and not until then, will someone biblically knowledgeable about end-times prophecy know the world has entered the Tribulation period. That is because all the signs are for events *within* the Tribulation, *not before* the Tribulation, and thus there are no signs in this dispensation for the rapture of the church or the Tribulation.

Some believe Matthew 24:40–41 speaks of the rapture of New Testament church dispensation believers, which would be a sign of the impending Tribulation. In the passage, one is taken and one is left. Above I said the one taken is taken in judgment, the one left behind enters the Davidic Messianic Kingdom. How can one know these passages speak of the Kingdom, not the rapture?

First, there is the context of the entire eschatological passage. Eschatology in the Synoptic gospels addresses Israel, the Tribulation, and the Kingdom. Second there is the passage itself. Jesus said conditions at the time of his return would be like the conditions in the days of Noah. The key phrase is that the unbelievers "did not know until the flood came and took them away." They did not know they would experience judgment, because they did not believe Noah's message. In Noah's day the unbeliever was taken in judgment by the flood and the believers—Noah and his family—were left behind to enter a new age. "So also will be the coming of the Son of Man." Of two in the field one will be taken in judgment and one left to enter the new kingdom age. Of two women grinding one will be taken in judgment and one left to enter the new kingdom age. This passage does not address the rapture of the New Testament church, and therefore gives no indication or sign for the coming Tribulation.

What The Bible Requires

Let us do what the Bible requires: live in the hope of Christ's return. In the Bible "hope" is a steadfast assurance that the thing hoped for will certainly come to pass. In the world we hope the weather will be good for the picnic: we are anxious about the weather. As Christians we hope Christ will return: we know he will. Live in that hope. We are also to be constantly prepared for the imminent rapture. John wrote, 1 John 3:3, that "everyone who has this hope [of Christ's return] purifies himself, just as Christ is pure." John didn't mean the hope itself was purifying. He meant that those who have this hope will continue to take action to keep themselves ready—living righteous lives of faith doing righteous works by faith. They will ignore the so-called "signs of the times" and keep themselves ready for the imminent, at-any-moment, return of Jesus Christ for his church at the rapture.

1 John 3:2, "Beloved ones, now children of God are we, and not yet revealed what we will be. We know that when he appears like him we will be, for we will see him as he is."

I have given this scripture as it literally appears in the Greek text. We might substitute nouns for pronouns to make the meaning clear.

> Beloved ones, now children of God are we, and not yet revealed what we will be. We know that when Christ appears like Christ we will be, for we will see Christ as he is.

There is a "now-yet future" aspect to the life of faith. For example, Abraham received the promises by faith, but full possession was yet-future, Hebrews 6:13–15; Hebrews 11:13–16, 39–40 (see my book, *A Private Commentary on the Book of Hebrews*). At Ephesians 1:3, the believer has as a present possession every spiritual blessing, but receives in this mortal life that portion which will be beneficial in living the Christian life.

The fullness of spiritual blessings awaits the believer in heaven; Ephesians 3:14–21 has that same perspective. At Ephesians 1:14, Paul recognizes the "now-yet future" aspect of the "redemption of the purchased possession." The souls of the Ephesians were fully redeemed, but their human nature and bodies were still corrupted and defiled by sin. The believer's human nature will be transformed and glorified at physical death or rapture (to remove the sin attribute), and his/her body will be transformed and glorified at the resurrection/rapture.

John says the believer is right now a child of God, but there is more to that position than can be realized during the believer's mortal life. The believer knows there is more, because the Scripture says there is more. The specific content of "more" cannot be fully defined at this time, 1 Corinthians 2:9.

The believer has assurance there will be something more when Jesus appears, because the believer will see Jesus just as he is. The veil of mortality will be gone. The curtain which even now prevents continuous unhindered communion—a curtain formed by the sin attribute in human nature and by acts of sinning—will be removed. Whether at physical death or at the rapture, the believer will see Jesus just as he is, because the believer will be just as Jesus is—not deity, but fully possessing the defining characteristics of the eternal life Christ has given us: to be fully and completely conformed to the image of Christ, Romans 8:29; Ephesians 1:5.

Paul describes the moment when the believer will see Jesus "just as he is" at Colossians 3:4. "Whenever Christ—your life—may be revealed, then also you along with him will be revealed in glory." At Philippians 3:21, Paul wrote that when Christ appears he will transform the believer's body to be like his glorious body.

Paul states the same a little differently at 1 Corinthians 15:35–54. In brief, at physical death the sin attribute will be removed from human nature, causing the saved soul to become sinless. The grace of indefectibility will be given, causing the saved soul to become incorruptible. The effects of sin, summed in the word "mortality," will be washed away from the soul: no more death and no more sin and no more disease and no more pain. Later the physical form will be recreated immortal and incorruptible (resurrection) and rejoined to the sinless, immortal, incorruptible soul to live forever the eternal life promised and given by Jesus Christ to his saved people.

As described by Paul and John, the believer will see, i.e., physically see, mentally know, and spiritually understand Jesus as he truly is: ascended, glorified, coming again, Prophet, Priest, Redeemer, and King. The specific content "will see him just as he is" is not described. The Scripture gives us glimpses. We know from Scripture that Jesus the Christ is the God-man; when we see him we will truly know that fact. We know Jesus is the Redeemer; in some way that fact will be more apparent. We know his glory is the glory of God, compare Revelation 4:8–11 with 5:9–14, but we will experience that glory in the fullest possible way. We know Jesus is King, but we will see him rule and rule with him, Revelation 1:6; 5:10; 1 Peter 2:9. And we know, as mentioned above (Colossians, Philippians, Corinthians) that we will be transformed to incorruptibility at Christ's appearing.

John continues

> 3 Now every person having this hope continually in Christ is constantly purifying himself, just as Christ is pure.

The hope of "having this hope continually in Christ" is the hope of Christ's return, 2:28, when he will be made visible, 3:2. The word translated "hope" is *elpís* [Zodhiates, s. v. 1680]. This is the only time *elpís* appears in John's writings, and it is important that its occurrence is associated with Christ's return. In other New Testament writings where *elpís* is associated with Christ's return, the word has the sense of absolute assurance, because Christ's return is certain. One could replace "hope" with "assurance" and not change the meaning.

The believer who is convicted Christ is returning continually lives by this knowledge (hope/assurance) with the result he/she is constantly taking action in the here and now to be morally pure just as Christ is morally pure. This is the work of the believer and the work of the Holy Spirit in the believer. It is growing in knowledge and grace, 2 Peter 3:18; growing in faith, patience, and wisdom, James 1:2–5; growing into spiritual maturity, 1 Corinthians 14:20; Philippians 3:15. The goal is when we see him to be able to stand before him with confidence and not be ashamed of the life we led, 1 John 2:28.

The verb "purifies" is *hagnízō*, to make clean, purify, consecrate [Zodhiates, s. v. 48]. The word was used in the LXX of ceremonial purification, for example, the priests washing to prepare for serving at the altar. The same sense occurs in the New Testament, e.g., John 11:55. But at 1 John 3:3, James 4:8, and 1 Peter 2:22 inward purification and dedication are the dominant idea, although the idea of outward purification is not excluded. Inward purification is moral purification: to be habitually righteous and loving.

Hagnízō is in the grammatical form present participle, giving the sense of an ongoing action. The believer is to continually take the actions necessary to be morally pure. He/she is to habitually practice righteousness: there are no exceptions to this rule. The emphasis is on choices: choose to say no to temptation; choose to do what is morally right toward self as well as toward others.

There is no contradiction between this verse and 1:7, "the blood of Jesus Christ his Son is continually cleansing us from every sin." Both are true. The scriptures everywhere describe God's grace as acting upon and with the believer. God's will is that by the power given through his grace the believer will take action to accomplish God's will.

The standard by which to measure the habitual practice of righteousness is Christ: "just as he is pure." The word "pure" is *hagnós*, freedom from defilements or impurities, to be morally pure, holy, perfect [Zodhiates, s. v. 53]. Why should the believer make every effort to live a morally pure life? So that when Christ appears he/she may have confidence and not be put to shame before him at his coming. How may the believer have confidence, not shame? By abiding in him, i.e., by living a morally pure life through the habitual practice of righteousness.

John presents the here-and-now practice of righteousness and moral purity in the eschatological setting of Christ's future return. The believer is to actively practice righteousness in order to become fully prepared in the here-and-now for the yet-future when you see Jesus.

There is a yet-future return by Christ to the air to remove his church from the earth, 1 Thessalonians 4:16–17; 2 Thessalonians 2:1; 1 Corinthians 15:51–53 (followed at a later time, nominally seven years, by the second advent of Christ with his church to the earth to receive his kingdom and commence his earthly rule, Revelation 19:11–20:6). John is speaking of that return to the air for the church (cf. John 14:2–3). How do we know this? Because a believer's state of confidence or shame "before him [standing in front of Christ] at his coming" indicates judgment, e.g., Romans 14:10. Paul speaks of the believer's judgment at 2 Corinthians 5:10; 1 Corinthians 3:12–15. This is not judgment for salvation (taken care of at the cross, Ephesians 2:8–9) but of reward or loss of reward for works practiced after salvation (Ephesians 2:10; Titus 2:14).

John's exhortation is to keep one's self morally pure in the light of Christ's return for his church. Unfortunately, many Christians are not keeping morally pure but are looking for signs of Christ's return. Looking for "signs of the times" is not a practice unique to modern times, but is as old as Christianity, cf. Acts 1:6; 2 Thessalonians 2:1–2. For example, Martin Luther (AD 1483–1546), and most Christians of his time, looked for signs. Luther even wrote a book on the subject in AD 1532, *The Signs of Christ's Coming and the Last Days*, because he thought the "signs of the times" indicated Christ's immediate return.

As previously mentioned, the New Testament church age is the last time before the end times. When this fact is combined with the imminent (at any moment) return of Christ to the air for his church—the *hárpazō*, the "catching away," aka: rapture—then we must say that there are no signs for the rapture; otherwise Christ's return for his church would not be imminent but predictable. Again, combining the fact the New Testament church age is last time before the end times, with the fact of Christ's at-any-moment return, one must say that the so-called signs are continuous, beginning from the moment Christ ascended, Acts 1:10, to now-present and yet-future days.

Put another way, no one, including Satan, knows when on God's calendar the rapture of the church will occur. No one, including Satan, knows when on God's calendar the Tribulation period will begin. No one, including Satan, knows when on God's calendar the second advent will occur. Therefore Satan always keeps the world ready for the tribulation and Christ's advent through wars, rumors of wars, and famine, and poverty, and epidemic diseases, and whatever brings political, economic, and social disruption to the world. Why does Satan do this? Because he does not know when. Therefore he is always prepared with some man to be his man of sin, his Antichrist, just in case any particular "today" is the day. Satan also is waiting for the rapture, for that is the next scheduled event on God's prophetic calendar.

So, yes, indeed, all the signs from Pentecost until now and into the future are signs the whole world is living in the last time before the end times. What is John's prescription for believers to cope during the last time?

> Abide in Christ, that when Christ appears we may have confidence, and not be put to shame before Christ at his coming . . . every person having this hope continually in Christ is constantly purifying himself, just as Christ is pure.

Don't look for Christ's coming at a particular day or season, because every sign will indicate he is coming and no sign will indicate when he will come. Instead, always be prepared for his at any moment coming to the air for his church.

(This chapter is an extract from *A Private Commentary on the Bible: John's Epistles*, beginning on p. 141, lightly edited to the present purpose.)

Appendix: The Rapture as a Jewish Wedding

Introduction

Explaining the rapture of the New Testament church by analogy to a Jewish betrothal-wedding has   gained in popularity. The essential elements are:

> After a Jewish betrothal, the analogy claims the bridegroom left to prepare a place for his fiancé and himself to live as husband and wife.

> This long separation afforded the fiancé time to gather her trousseau and prepare for married life.

> After a long time the groom returns, marries his betrothed, and then takes her to the new home he prepared.

> Christ left, is preparing a place, and is returning to receive the NT church to himself at the rapture. Therefore the rapture is like a Jewish betrothal-wedding.

Does the comparison of the rapture with a Jewish betrothal-wedding conform to what the Bible presents about the New Testament church and the rapture of the New Testament church? No. The rapture as Jewish betrothal-wedding is the misuse of historical-cultural information, an allegorical interpretation of certain Scriptures, and an improper use of certain figures of speech, each of which fails to conform to the proper use of the Literal hermeneutic.

The Literal hermeneutic requires understanding Scripture within the historical-cultural context of the biblical setting, and an interpretation of the scriptures that considers the literary context in which those scriptures are set. The Literal hermeneutic also has definite rules concerning the proper interpretation and use of figures of speech. The purpose of this article is to show the rapture-as-Jewish-betrothal-wedding analogy does not meet the high standards of the Literal hermeneutic.

Let me pause and say the rapture of the New Testament church is a biblical fact. How do we know? The Literal hermeneutic teaches the removal of the New Testament church from the world by Christ at some yet-future date. The fact of the rapture is found by comparing Scripture with Scripture: John 14:2–3; 1 Thessalonians 4:13–17; Revelation

3:10. The fact of the rapture is not in doubt, only the allegorical rapture-as-Jewish-betrothal-wedding is disputed. Now to the argument.

Historical-Cultural Information

What historical-cultural information is used to support the rapture as Jewish betrothal-wedding ? Usually it is data similar to that found in the *Jewish Encyclopedia*.

> After the lapse of a certain period from the time of betrothal (twelve months if the bride was a virgin and a minor, and thirty days if she was an adult or a widow; Sefaria, *Ketubot*, 57b), during which the bride could prepare her trousseau, the marriage proper was celebrated. This was attended with the ceremony of home-taking (*likkuhin* or *nissu'in*) and isolation of the bridal pair in the bridal chamber (*huppah*). From that time they became husband and wife, even if there was no cohabitation. Various ceremonies attended the act of marriage (see Marriage Ceremony). An important feature was the handing over of the marriage contract (*ketubah*) to the bride. In later times the two stages of marriage were combined, a custom universally followed at the present time. [http://www.jewishencyclopedia.com/articles/10435-marriage-laws]

The problem with this data? It does not meet the requirement of the Literal hermeneutic. The marriage custom described is a 6th century AD Jewish custom, not a 1st century AD custom. The above quote, used by proponents of the analogy, is from the Babylonian Talmud, written ca. AD 450–550.

There is historical-cultural data closer to the time of Jesus. The Mishnah was compiled ca. 200 BC–AD 200, and therefore is more likely to be the betrothal-wedding rules Christ would have referred to—if Christ had proposed a rapture-as-Jewish-betrothal-wedding analogy. However, the Mishnah knows nothing of a *mandatory* waiting period between betrothal and marriage. The word "betrothal" occurs seventeen times in the Mishnah [Danby. *Mishnah*, 815]. The Mishnah has many varied rules about betrothal (see tractate, *Kiddushin*), but none present any kind of mandatory waiting period between betrothal and marriage.

When we turn to the tractate on marriage, *Ketuboth*, the Mishnah does say, "After the husband has demanded her, a virgin is granted twelve months wherein to provide for herself; and like as [such time] is granted to the woman so it is granted to the man to provide for himself. And a widow [is granted] thirty days" [M. *Ketuboth*, 5.2]. The waiting period was not mandatory, and need not continue for twelve months.

Under what we assume, from the Mishnah, was current Jewish law in 1st century Israel, a young woman could be betrothed when she was twelve years and one day old. The law reads, "A man may give his daughter in betrothal while she is still in her girlhood" [M., *Kiddushin*, 2.1]. The translation "girlhood" is the Hebrew *na'ărâ*, defined as twelve years and a day old or older, unmarried but marriageable. (A woman who had reached her majority was described as *bogereth*.) The fact a twelve year old could be betrothed was probably the reason the Mishnah allowed, but did not require, a twelve month period to elapse between betrothal and marriage. Puberty was more likely at age thirteen than at age twelve.

Summing up. During the time Jesus walked the earth, it seems likely twelve months was allowed between betrothal and marriage, if the girl was a virgin. But not if the woman was a widow. The twelve month period can only be declared, "seems likely," because the historical document Mishnah was compiled between 200 BC–AD 200, a sufficient span of time to cast doubt on when that particular custom came into existence. Regardless, delaying the marriage until the expiration of the allowable waiting period between the betrothal and wedding was not mandatory, only customary.

The Babylonian Talmud (*Ketubot*, 57b) also did not mandate twelve months elapse from betrothal to marriage when it said, "a virgin is given twelve months to prepare for her marriage." Contemporary rabbinical comments present the historical understanding of the custom. The rabbis opined the reason for the twelve months was for her to complete puberty; to go from *na'ărâ* to *bogereth*.

For example, "Rabbi Zeira said: It was taught in the Tosefta, Ketubot 5:1 (the *Tofseta* is from the same time period as the Mishnah). with regard to a minor girl: Either she or her father may delay the wedding until she has reached majority" [Babylonian Talmud, Ketubot, 57b]. So, not a mandatory twelve months, but only sufficient time to complete the transition of puberty. Puberty is considered completed after the first menses. Then the *na'ărâ* has reached reproductive maturity and become a *bogereth*.

"Rabbi Abba bar Levi said, "One may not finalize an agreement to marry a minor girl in order to marry her while she is still a minor, but one may finalize an agreement to marry a minor girl in order to marry her when she becomes an adult woman" [Babylonian Talmud, Ketubot, 57b]. Here the duration depends on the completion of puberty.

"Rabbi Huna said, "If she has reached her majority, even for just one day, and then she is betrothed, she is given her thirty days to prepare for her wedding, like a widow, since prior to reaching adulthood she presumably had already prepared everything needed for her marriage" [Babylonian Talmud, Ketubot, 57b]. Here the waiting period is thirty days if puberty has been completed.

The Rabbis interpreted the grant of twelve months to apply to those who had been betrothed before the completion of puberty. To make a general application of that rule to Christ and the New Testament church seems unwarranted. (I think we can all agree the NT church is not in the process of puberty.)

Conclusion: the 6th century historical source used as the basis for the rapture-as-Jewish-betrothal-wedding analogy is not only *not* the historically current rule for the time of Jesus, but also had a limited application. The waiting period was to allow for the completion of puberty. If puberty was completed the waiting period was limited to thirty days. The same seems true of the instructions in the Mishnah. Moreover, the New Testament church is not a *na'ărâ*, and is not in transition through puberty, so the "waiting period" rule cannot rationally apply to the New Testament church, even allegorically. No one using the rapture-as-Jewish-betrothal-wedding allegory suggests the New Testament church is in puberty from Pentecost to the rapture.

Scriptures

There are several biblical issues with the rapture as Jewish betrothal-wedding analogy. The first is, we don't know that much about Jewish betrothal-wedding customs in first century Israel. All our knowledge assumes the rules in the Mishnah were in use during Jesus' earthly ministry. The gospels have nothing to say about the relationship between betrothal and marriage—are not the gospels the primary source for the rapture-wedding analogy? Either Jesus put his departure and return for the church in terms of a Jewish betrothal-wedding, or he did not. The Scriptures say he did not.

There is no mention of betrothal customs in the gospels, meaning neither the writer nor Jesus said anything about betrothal customs. We see one mention of a betrothal in the gospels: Mary was betrothed to Joseph, Luke 1:27. Jesus did not describe his relationship with his church as a betrothal. Jesus did not use or refer to what we know of betrothal customs as stated in the then historically current document, the Mishnah.

Did Jesus speak about the act of marriage following a betrothal? No. Did Jesus speak of the period of time between a betrothal and marriage? No. Jesus said marriage was between a man and a woman, Matthew 19:5; Mark 10:8–9. That's it, nothing more (he did speak about divorce). Jesus did not refer to his relationship with the New Testament church as a betrothal or as a marriage.

The validity of the "rapture-Jewish wedding" analogy depends on the answer to a simple question: Do the Scriptures present Jesus the Christ as betrothed to the New Testament church? The answer may be developed from several points of view. First point of view: the relationship between Christ and the New Testament church is created by what is known as the New Covenant.

The New covenant is first stated in Jeremiah 31:31–33. The covenant promises YHWH will, "put My law in their [those of national ethnic Israel who are members of the covenant] minds, and write it on their hearts; and I will be their God, and they shall be My people. No more shall every man teach his neighbor, and every man his brother, saying, 'Know the Lord,' for they all shall know Me, from the least of them to the greatest of them, says the Lord. For I will forgive their iniquity, and their sin I will remember no more."

The New Covenant in Jeremiah is yet-future for Israel, "behold, the days are coming." (As a Dispensationalist I believe the New covenant for Israel waits for the Millennial Kingdom.) The key fact in relation to this discussion is the New Covenant is not a marriage covenant. YHWH does say Israel broke the Mosaic covenant, "though I was a husband to them," but the Mosaic covenant is nowhere described as a marriage covenant. (I will address the "husband" figure of speech below.)

The word "husband" in Jeremiah 31:32 cannot have been used in a literal sense. YHWH is not a man that he should marry. Nor does the New covenant refer to betrothal or marriage. The word "husband" is used figuratively of the fidelity YHWH showed toward Israel, even though Israel was faithless and broke the Mosaic Covenant. One of the rules for interpreting a figure of speech is, "A figure of speech is not used to teach the literal thing on which it is based." YHWH illustrating his Mosaic covenant relationship with Israel as a husband is not being used to teach YHWH is literally a husband to Israel.

Figures of Speech

I believe it necessary at this point to divert from the main topic to discuss the proper use and interpretation of biblical figures of speech, because the wedding-as-rapture depends heavily on an improper interpretation of figures. There are five unbreakable, unalterable, unchanging rules for figures of speech [Quiggle, *Literal Hermeneutic*, 28–29]:

> A figure of speech is a comparison (by example or analogy) of one thing with another that clarifies some aspect of the thing being illustrated by the figure of speech.

> A figure of speech does not teach doctrine. A figure of speech clarifies what is being taught for the purpose of helping the understanding.

> A figure of speech clarifies one aspect, not all aspects, of the thing being illustrated.

> A figure of speech is based in something literal and is intended to teach something literal.

> A figure of speech does not teach the literal thing on which it is based.

The rule that is of interest to the rapture-as-Jewish-betrothal-wedding analogy is the last, "A figure of speech does not teach the literal thing on which it is based."

The use of marriage is a biblical figure of speech designed to communicate the idea of spiritual fidelity, and nothing more. In relation to the figure of speech, "YHWH as husband to Israel" (or the more common, "Israel as wife of YHWH"), the covenant at the time Jeremiah wrote, the Mosaic covenant, was not a marriage covenant. God and the people of Israel did not become one-flesh, Genesis 2:23–24.

The figurative use of marriage was created by God through his prophets to communicate the nation Israel, as a whole, was religiously unfaithful to YHWH; hence the corresponding use of adultery to describe Israel's idolatry. Only false gods marry—ask the Egyptians, the Greeks, the Romans, the Mormons. The one true God does not present himself as married, literally or metaphorically, because "God is not a man." Marriage as a metaphor or illustration does not teach God is literally married, but that Israel was spiritually unfaithful.

Let us examine the use of fire, a well-known figure of speech. Literal fire destroys, and literal fire cleanses. A literal fire will consume a building. A literal fire will purge impurities from ore (smelting). From these two literal uses of literal fire the scriptures teach two literal meanings: judging the unsaved and cleansing the saved. For example, absolutely no one properly using the Literal hermeneutic will interpret, e.g., Isaiah 30:27, "And His [YHWH's] tongue is like a burning fire," to mean YHWH's tongue is literally burning up Assyria. The figure of speech is a simile: YHWH will destroy Assyria as a fire destroys a building. The imagery is the word of God in the mouth of God pronouncing judgment on the enemy of God.

No one properly using the Literal hermeneutic will interpret Revelation 1:16, a sharp two-edged sword comes out of Christ's mouth, to mean Christ walks around with a sword coming out of his mouth. Nor will the interpreter say it means Christ's tongue is metaphorically razor sharp like a sword and metaphorically cuts the listener. The two edged sword is a figure of speech used as an illustration of the Word of God at work in the believer and the world, Hebrews 4:12, revealing and convicting. This figure of speech as used in Revelation represents the Word of God in the mouth of God accomplishing the will of God. The interpretation, when all aspects of Christ's visual appearance are considered, is Christ the high priest come to judge his people, Revelation 2, 3, and God the righteous Judge coming to judge the world, Revelation 6–19, compare 19:15, "From His mouth comes a sharp sword, so that with it He may strike down the nations."

Is the New Testament Church the Bride of Christ?

Israel was not literally the wife of YHWH under the Mosaic covenant, and will not literally be the wife of YHWH under the yet-future New covenant; neither was a marriage covenant. Even so, the New Testament church is never presented literally or metaphorically as the bride or wife of Christ.

Do the Scriptures say the New Testament Church is the Bride of Christ?

Another diversion from the main subject is required. Reformed theology allegorically interprets the Scripture in order to claim the New Testament church is the Bride of Christ. Why Reformed theology does so is unimportant to this article (it is based in part on the Reformed replacement doctrine: OT Israel was the wife of YHWH; YHWH divorced OT Israel; the New Testament church is now Israel.) What is important is this Reformed allegory has become so accepted as genuine Christian doctrine that it is rarely questioned. What does the Scripture say—or not say?

Jesus *never* names the New Testament church as his bride. Jesus *never* describes his return for the New Testament church in terms of a Jewish betrothal-wedding. In fact, the New Testament view of the church is quite different from that of a bride:

John 10:27, "my sheep."

Hebrews 2:10, "having brought many sons to glory."

Hebrews 2:11, "he is not ashamed to call them brothers."

Hebrews 2:13, "Look, I and the children whom God has given to me."

Sheep, sons, brothers, children, are all illustrative of the salvific relationship. The Scripture never names the New Testament church as a bride or wife.

I hear the objection, "what about the bride of Christ in Ephesians 5?" Tell me, show me, quote to me the verse in Ephesians 5 where the New Testament church is named a bride. The word does not appear in Ephesians 5. What is Ephesians 5 all about? Human marriage. Not betrothal, not Christ leaving and returning, not the rapture of the church. Only human marriage is in view. Let's look:

> Just as Christ is the head of the church, so the husband is head of the wife, v. 23.

> Just as the church is subject to Christ, so the wife is subject to the husband, v. 34.

> Just as Christ loves the church, so the husband is to love the wife, v. 25

The comparisons here are leadership, authority-submission, and love. The comparisons are an illustration in the form of a simile: a simple comparison of dissimilar things using the words like or as. The comparison is not Christ to husband, church to wife, but leadership (or submission-authority, or love) in the husband-wife relationship is to be a similar nature as that in the Christ-church relationship [Quiggle, *Ephesians*, 372ff.].

Christ is the leader of the church, the church is in submission to Christ's authority, and Christ loves the church. Christ's relation to his church is being used to illustrate certain aspects of the husband-wife relationship. The husband is the leader of the wife, the wife is in submission to the husband's authority, the husband is to love his wife. "Just as Christ and the church. . . even so the husband and wife" in the areas of leadership, authority-submission, and love. The comparison does not teach the church is the wife or the bride of Christ. Nor is it required for the church to be the wife or bride of Christ for the comparison to be valid.

The members of the New Testament church are, "members of Christ's body," Ephesians 5:30. This is again a comparison. What is in view is the exclusive-loyalty covenant that is human marriage, Genesis 2:24–25. The husband and wife do not literally become one bone, one flesh but they do become an exclusive partnership. The husband and wife exclusively commit themselves to one another in the physical, emotional, and spiritual aspects of their relationship to the benefit and enjoyment of one another and none else.

Even so Christ and the believer. Human marriage, as defined at Genesis 2:24–25, and used at Ephesians 5:31, is being used as an illustration of the exclusivity of the spiritual union and personal commitment between the believer and Christ. That union and commitment is a spiritual union between Christ and the believer through the indwelling Holy Spirit. The illustration as used in Ephesians 5 does not teach marriage between the church and Christ and does not teach betrothal between the church and Christ. Nowhere in Ephesians does Paul state the New Testament church is the wife or bride of Christ. The word "bride" never appears.

There are two verses might seem to imply the church is the wife of Christ.

One verse that may seem to speak of a marriage yet to occur is Ephesians 5:27. "In order that he should present to himself the church in glory, not having spot or wrinkle or any of such things, but that it should be holy and without blemish." That is not an illustration of marriage, because in marriage the groom does not present his bride to himself. What this is, is explained in 5:25–26, "The husbands are to love their wives, even just as Christ loved the church and gave up himself for her, so that he might sanctify her, having cleansed her by the washing of water with the Word." That is redemption and sanctification, not marriage. Christ presents the church to himself through his actions of redemption and sanctification. In 5:27 neither betrothal nor wedding are mentioned or in view. In 5:26–27 the comparison is "love" not betrothal or wedding.

Paul quoting Genesis 2:24 at Ephesians 5:31 may seem to imply a marital relationship between Christ and the church. Even if one accepts that interpretation, the quote is not about betrothal, a bride, a wedding, or a rapture, but the character of the husband-wife marital relationship. But as I just explained (above) Genesis is quoted because it describes the exclusive nature of the believer's relationship with Christ.

The point of quoting Genesis 2:24 in Ephesians 5 is unity, fidelity, loyalty. Submit to your husband's leadership as the church submits to Christ. Love your wife as Christ loves the church. Nourish and cherish your wife as Christ does the church. The point is the character of the relationship between husband and wife is to be of the same character as the relationship between Christ and the New Testament church. Not betrothal, not bride, not wife, but love, respect, and care for one another.

Looking to Genesis 2:24, the New Testament church is not literally

Christ's flesh and bones. Just as the husband and wife are not literally "one flesh." The sinner leaves his old life and transfers his loyalty to Christ. The husband leaves his old life and transfers his loyalty to the wife. The husband's loyalty prior to marriage was to his parents. In marriage the husband transfers that loyalty to his wife, ad she transfers her loyalty to her husband. That is what "one flesh means": the union between husband and wife is created by an exclusive loyalty contract. "Marriage," and "bride" (if these words occurred in the Ephesians passage), and "wife," when used as a figure of speech in relation to God, is always about unity, loyalty, and fidelity.

Someone somewhere looks to the Lamb's wedding supper at Revelation 19:7. The "Lamb's wife" in that passage is the New Testament church *only if* you import that concept into the passage and *then* "discover" it there. The New Testament church is not mentioned by name in the passage. What is more likely in this book about the consummation of God's eschatological program, which began in the Old Testament and is complete in the New Testament, is the "Lamb's wife" is all the saved in both Testaments, from Adam to the end of the Tribulation. Christ is about to return to the earth to establish the Davidic-Messianic kingdom promised to national ethnic Israel. That act will be the consummation of all the Old Testament kingdom promises, not the promises to the New Testament church. The New Testament church participates in the Davidic-Messianic-Millennial Kingdom as joint-heirs with Christ, Romans 8:17. The "lamb's wife" in Revelation 19:7 is the eschatological kingdom and its members, including the New Testament church.

Returning to the Main Subject

The New Testament church is not the bride of Christ, whether literally or in a figure of speech. Therefore the rapture as Jewish betrothal-wedding fails the test of Scripture. The New Testament church has a New covenant with Christ. Some believe it is a current application of YHWH's yet-future, Jeremiah 31:31–34, New covenant with Israel. Others, like myself, believe Christ's covenant with the New Testament church is similar to YHWH's New covenant with Israel, but independent of it, being a covenant between Christ and the New Testament church. The conditions of Christ's New covenant with the New Testament church are similar to that of YHWH with Israel,

Hebrews 10:16–17. I believe they are two similar but independent covenants for two separate people groups to accomplish the same end for both people groups. National ethnic Israel and the New Testament church are distinct people groups in God's economy, with similar, but individual, destinies.

Regardless of which view one takes, just like YHWH's New covenant with Israel is not a marriage contract, even so Christ's New covenant with the New Testament church is not a marriage contract. It is a covenant promising salvation and regeneration—a covenant of redemption.

There is no place in the New Testament where Christ's covenant relationship with his church is described in terms of a betrothal or marriage. But someone somewhere will point to New Testament use of marriage to make the opposite case (as does the rapture-wedding analogy). Let's take a look.

There are two literal weddings in the New Testament. One is the wedding at Cana, John 2, a marriage celebration. At this stage of Jesus' public ministry, he is announcing "the Kingdom of Heaven is at hand." Jesus' activities at the Cana wedding are in relation to his messianic mission to Israel. Wine is used as a figure of joy in Messiah's Kingdom, e.g., Jeremiah 31:12; Hosea 14:7; Amos 9:13–14.

A wedding is not a prominent Old Testament messianic theme, but marriage is occasionally used as a figure of speech of the relationship between Messiah and national ethnic Israel. See Isaiah 54:1; 62:4; Jeremiah 3:14; Hosea 2:19–20. Jesus used marriage as a figure of speech to describe his messianic relationship with Israel at Matthew 22:1–4; 25:1–3. But in no place does Jesus use marriage to describe his relationship with the New Testament church.

The second marriage in the New Testament is that between Joseph and Mary. In this marriage story, Mary leaves the village after the betrothal, for three months, Joseph stays behind, and when Mary returns she receives Joseph as her husband. Nothing in this betrothal-marriage supports the "rapture-Jewish wedding" theory.

Other gospel references to Jewish weddings are not literal weddings. In John 3, John Baptist uses marriage figuratively to describe his decreasing importance in the proclamation of the messianic kingdom: the groomsman becomes less important when the bridegroom arrives. Applying the Literal hermeneutic, which views the historical-cultural aspects of the passage, no one hearing the Baptist describe Christ as a bridegroom would have thought of the non-existent New Testament church; inserting the idea into the passage is an excellent example of an anachronistic interpretation. But, to play the game (so-to-speak), if Christ was being presented by the Baptist as a literal bridegroom—which he was not—then two observations: one, the moment is not about betrothal, nor returning for the bride, but is about the marriage ceremony; two, the bride would have been national ethnic Israel, not the non-existent New Testament church. However, the figure was not about betrothal or marriage, but John Baptist. A figure of speech does not teach the literal thing on which it is based.

Matthew 9:15–17 (parallels Mark 2:19; Luke 5:34) uses "bridegroom" in a figurative manner. The point of the parable is Mosaic Judaism was not part of the coming kingdom of national ethnic Israel under the Messiah. The message at this early stage of Jesus' ministry is about the promised Davidic-Messianic kingdom, because the kingdom is still being proclaimed. As with the Baptist's use of the same figure, the moment is not about betrothal, nor returning for the bride; and if a bride was in view (which it is not) the bride would have been national ethnic Israel, not the non-existent New Testament church. The "bridegroom taken away" is a reference to the coming crucifixion. No mention is made of a return. Nor can the figure be about Christ ascending into heaven, else he would have condemned the New Testament church to perpetual mourning until his return.

Matthew 25 uses a bridegroom as an element of a parable. Before continuing, a few words about interpreting a parable.

> A parable is a story—a word picture or an illustration—told to teach a single point. A parable is usually built with something literal (a farmer sowing seed, a man giving a banquet), but may also use figures of speech, idioms, slang, symbols, or types. Like a symbol, a parable is always based in something literal and always teaches something literal. The intent of a parable is not to describe every aspect of doctrine, but only to illustrate one point. Before trying to interpret a parable, look for the reason for telling the parable, and there you will usually find the one, single, main point the parable is teaching. Do not try to interpret

all the parts that were used to build the parable. The parts are the cart and horse that carries the one main point. [Quiggle, *The Literal Hermeneutic*, 36.]

Whenever any interpreter seeks an elaboration of meaning in a parable, and commences to find meaning in far more points than the parable can hope to make, that interpreter has returned to the reprehensible method of allegorizing the parables. [Ramm, 279].

The point of the parable of Matthew 9:15–17 is national ethnic Israel's preparedness for Messiah. Here the timing is the second advent, not the rapture. In the parable the marriage ceremony has already taken place, the husband is bringing his wife to his home. No rapture, no waiting period, no betrothal are in this parable. But the point *is not* the marriage. The returning husband and wife are simply an element on which the story is built, part of the cart and horse carrying the message. The point of the parable is, will Israel be prepared when Messiah returns to establish the kingdom? This parable has nothing do to with the rapture of the New Testament church.

No verse in the Four Gospels teaches the rapture is like a Jewish wedding.

But let us assume the point for a moment. There are doctrinal problems. A Jewish marriage consisted of two stages, betrothal and wedding. In the scenario imagined by the analogy, Christ paid the purchase price for the New Testament church, left, and is coming back for the wedding.

Let's take a moment to more closely examine the idea Christ purchased the church. In a Jewish betrothal the prospective groom often gave money establish the betrothal, "By three means is the woman acquired . . . She is acquired by money, or by writ, or by intercourse" [M. *Kiddushin*, 1.1]. Acts 20:28 reads in a few versions, "the church of God which he purchased with his own blood." However, the word translated "purchased" in the KJV, ASV, NKJV, HCSB, *peripoiéō* [Zodhiates, s. v. 4046], means "to acquire," not purchase. The verse is properly translated (and with a little paraphrasing), "the church of God which Christ acquired through his propitiatory death." (The word blood in Acts 20:28 is a euphemism for death.) Christ's death propitiated God for sin, 1 John 2:2, Romans 3:25. The merit of the propitiatory death is applied to sinners through the decree of election (Ephesians 1:4) and the gift of God (Ephesians 2:8).

That salvation of the soul effected by the gift of God is a completed salvation. We know this for two reasons. One, the soul of every saved sinner is regenerated, born-again. Two, every physically dead sinner goes to heaven to be in God's presence, and is certain to experience reunification with the resurrected physical body.

So one of the doctrinal problems with the rapture-as-Jewish-betrothal-wedding analogy is in the analogy salvation corresponds to the betrothal stage. The consequence of salvation as betrothal is an incomplete salvation—a betrothal is not a marriage, it is the promise of a marriage, even in first century Jewish culture. A Jewish marriage consisted of two stages: betrothal, then wedding. One without the other was incomplete. The betrothed woman was not a wife. The Jewish betrothal laws treated her legally as a wife in one aspect only: the betrothal could only be dissolved by a divorce.

This is a very troubling aspect of the analogy. Christ on the cross propitiated God for the sins of the world, 1 John 2:2; Romans 3:25. The merit of that propitiation is applied through the degree of election by the gift of God (Ephesians 2:8) to effect the complete redemption of the soul. We know the redemption of the soul is complete because the soul is regenerated, born-again, and goes to heaven upon physical death. But if, as the analogy suggests—indeed, as it must proclaim—the soul is only betrothed to Christ, then the soul is waiting for the rapture-wedding to complete its salvation. The rapture-as-Jewish-betrothal-wedding analogy teaches an incomplete salvation.

In fact, the rapture-as-Jewish-betrothal-wedding analogy implies some sort of purgatory for the physically dead believer (only the completely saved go to heaven) until salvation is completed by the rapture-wedding—God forbid.

Regeneration indicates salvation is not like a betrothal waiting for the wedding, but is a completed salvation. That condition of born-again-regenerated applies equally to the Old Testament saved sinner, who will not be raptured. As one of the Puritans (Charnock, 12) said (a truth apparently not known today in Reformed theology), "It is absolutely necessary that all should be new born . . . no age, no time excludes it." The redemption of the soul is complete, and viewed as completed, even though the body remains to be redeemed, Ephesians 1:14, through resurrection. Just as the Old Testament saints were not waiting for their salvation to be completed, even so the New Testament saints are not waiting for a rapture-wedding to complete their salvation. The rapture-as-Jewish-betrothal-wedding analogy implicitly distorts the completed nature of salvation.

Eschatology

The analogy depends on a certain eschatology. The eschatology of the Synoptics is not applicable to the rapture as Jewish betrothal-wedding theme. That eschatology is the Tribulation, the second advent ending the Tribulation, and the consequent Davidic-Messianic-Millennial Kingdom. As Pentecost stated,

> [A] fourth view suggests that verses 4–8 outline the first half of the tribulation and verses 9-26 describe the second half of the week . . . Consistency of interpretation would seem to eliminate any application of this portion of Scripture to the church or the church age. Inasmuch as the Lord is dealing with the prophetic program for Israel . . . The parallelism between verses 4-8 and Revelation 6 seems to indicate that the first half of the Tribulation is here described. [Pentecost, 278.]

Pentecost quotes Arno C. Gaebelein and E. Schuyler English in support [Pentecost, 278]. This must also have been Pentecost's view, for he speaks approvingly.

The eschatology in John's gospel only seems applicable to the analogy. The only eschatology in John's Gospel is at 14:2–3. There, Jesus states, "In my Father's house are many abiding places; but if not I would have said that to you. I go to prepare a place for you. And when I should go and prepare a place for you, I am coming again and will receive you to myself; that where I am, you may be also."

That is the only gospel reference to the rapture. But let us be careful not to add to what Jesus said. Jesus did not say, "Just like a bridegroom leaving to prepare a place for his bride, so I go to prepare a place for you," etc. There is no mention of a betrothal or a wedding. The only way to find a reference to Jewish marriage (betrothal plus wedding) in the eschatology of the gospels is to bring it with you so you can "discover" it there.

Conclusion

The rapture as Jewish betrothal-wedding is an allegorical interpretation created by overlaying that analogy on top of certain scriptures in order to support a doctrine decided beforehand. Here is the thesis:

> The New Testament portrays the Church as the Bride of Christ in Ephesians 5:22-33 (Paul even quotes Genesis 2:24 as the union at the Parousia of the Bridegroom in v.31!); cf. Romans 7:4; 2 Corinthians 11:2; James 4:4. In the opening verses of John 14, the marriage covenant is confirmed. Paul continually reminds us of the purchase price and the covenant by which we, the Bride, are set apart, or sanctified.
>
> https://www.khouse.org/articles/2003/449/?fbclid=IwAR3btcTBTO2iZDOnU82MwyL5-ZYoZRDBQxDHpALSeWgkeOilBxXEv5Q9xOg

No, the New Testament church is never identified by Paul as a bride or wife of Christ. Genesis 2:24 is about the exclusive loyalty covenant that is marriage, to illustrate the exclusive loyalty required of the believer toward Christ. No New Testament scripture ever creates a marriage contract between the New Testament church and Christ. Christ did not pay a "purchase price" for the church, he propitiated God for sin so God could act redemptively toward sinners, thereby acquiring the church through his propitiatory death. The opening verses of John 14 say nothing about betrothal, or marriage, or a wedding. Like most allegorical interpretations, this view manipulates the Scriptures to "discover" the doctrine decided upon beforehand.

Is Jesus returning for the New Testament church in an event named in the Greek text of 1 Thessalonians 4:17 the *hárpazō*, the "catching away," and in the Latin text the *raptuare*, the rapture. Yes. How do we know? John 14:2–3; 1 Thessalonians 4:13–17; Revelation 3:10. Does the rapture correspond to a 4th century AD description of the two aspects of Jewish marriage as practiced in the 6th century AD? No. Does the New Testament teach the rapture is like a Jewish betrothal-wedding? No. Does the Bible ever identify the New Testament church as the bride of Christ? No. Step away from the allegorical interpretive method; don't play with it, it will only hurt you.

Appendix: Is Enoch a Type of the Rapture?

Is Enoch, Genesis 5:21–23, a type of the rapture of the New Testament church? Some think so, drawing an analogy between Enoch and the Rapture.

Let us biblically consider the analogy between Enoch and the rapture of the New Testament church. Enoch was translated into heaven because he walked with God. He lived a manner of life (walk) pleasing to God, and as a reward was removed to heaven (and as a mercy, for in being translated that righteous man did not have to endure another 600 years of the world's increasing sinfulness). He would have died before the flood, an important point, had God allowed him to continue on the earth.

If Enoch's translation into heaven is a picture of the rapture of the New Testament church, then only those believers whose lives are pleasing to God will be removed into heaven. That "he pleased God" was the condition for his translation into heaven, even as those who support this analogy will state, quoting Hebrews 11:5.

This analogy between Enoch and the Rapture is nothing less than the "Partial Rapture" theory, which states, members of the New Testament church are raptured as they become pleasing to God, meaning some believers will not endure the Tribulation, but others will endure the Tribulation, until they have suffered enough to be pleasing.

Let us apply the author's analogy to another man of the times who pleased God. Noah, Genesis 6:9, "Noah walked with God." But Noah wasn't translated out of the world. Noah, who was safe in the ark, nevertheless endured through the time of God's wrath against the world, a "Tribulation" of worldwide proportions. Does that mean Noah is a type of the rapture of the New Testament church? If so, then the New Testament church will endure through the Tribulation and be raptured at the end, a post-tribulational rapture.

I reject this analogy. The entire living New Testament church will be raptured out of the world prior to the Tribulation, whether living pleasing to God, or not. It is the propitiation of Christ to God for all the believer's sins, not a pleasing manner of life, which ensures the removal of all New Testament church at the same time: a pre-Tribulation rapture.

159

Enoch illustrates a partial rapture, but others were also walking pleasing to God: a whole chapter of believers pleasing to God, but God did not translate them. So there is not a Partial rapture, not a Post-tribulation rapture. The Bible student must beware of analogies built on one expression or phrase that doesn't consider the entire biblical context, but manipulates that context to support a pre-determined theory.

Sources

Aharoni, Yohanan, and Michael Avi-Yohan. *The MacMillan Bible Atlas*. Rev. New York, NY: 1968.

Boettner, Loraine. *The Millennium*. Philadelphia, PA: The Presbyterian and Reformed Publishing Co., 1958.

Bromiley, G. W., ed. *International Standard Bible Encyclopedia*. 4 vols. Rev. Grand Rapids, MI: Eerdmans Publishing, 1988.

Burton, Ernest De Witt. *The Epistle to the Galatians*. The International Critical Commentary. Edinburgh: T. & T. Clark, 1921.

Charnock, Stephen. *The Doctrine of Regeneration*. Grand Rapids, MI: Baker Book House, 1980.

Danby, Herbert. *The Mishnah*. Oxford, England: Oxford University Press, 1933.

Eadie, John. *The John Eadie Greek Text Commentaries*. 5 vols. 1869. Reprinted, Grand Rapids, MI: Baker Book House, 1979.

Fruchtenbaum, Arnold G. *Israelology: The Missing Link in Systematic Theology*. Tustin, CA: Ariel Ministries, 1989.

Harris et al., R. Laird, and Gleason L. Archer Jr., and Bruce K. Waltke. *Theological Wordbook of the Old Testament*. 2 vols. Chicago, IL: Moody Press, 1980.

Harrison, Everett, F., ed. *Baker's Dictionary of Theology*. Grand Rapids, MI: Baker Book House, 1960.

Hogg, C. F., and W. E. Vine. *The Epistle to the Galatians*. Grand Rapids, MI: Kregel Publications, 1921.

Kittel, Gerhard, and Gerhard Friedrich. *Theological Dictionary of the New Testament*. 10 vols. Translated by Geoffrey W. Bromiley. Grand Rapids, MI: Eerdmans Publishing, 1967.

Longenecker, Richard, N. *Galatians*. Word Biblical Commentary. Vol. 41. Waco, TX: Word Books, 1990.

McClain, Alva J. *The Greatness of the Kingdom*. 1968. Reprinted, Winona Lake, IN: BMH Books, 1974.

Pentecost, J. Dwight. *Things to Come. A Study in Biblical Eschatology*. Grand Rapids, MI: Zondervan, 1958.

Quiggle, James D. *A Private Commentary on the Epistle to the*

Ephesians. CreateSpace, 2011.

_____ . *A Private Commentary on the Bible: Revelation 1–7.* Amazon/KDP, 2022.

_____ . *A Private Commentary on the Bible: Thessalonians.* Amazon/KDP, 2021.

_____ . *Antichrist, His Genealogy, Kingdom, and Religion.* Self-published, 2011.

_____ . *Biblical Essays.* Amazon/KDP, 2018.

_____ . *Biblical Essays II.* Amazon/KDP, 2019.

_____ . *Biblical Essays III.* Amazon/KDP, 2020.

_____ . *Biblical Essays IV.* Amazon/KDP, 2021.

_____ . *Dictionary of Doctrinal Words.* Amazon/KDP, 2018.

_____ . *Dispensational Eschatology, An Explanation and Defense of the Doctrine.* Amazon/KDP, 2013.

_____ . *God Became Incarnate.* Amazon/KDP, 2014.

_____ . *Life, Death, Eternity.* Amazon/KDP, 2019.

_____ . *The Literal Hermeneutic, Explained and Illustrated.* Amazon/KDP, 2018, 2020.

_____ . *Thirty-Six Essentials of the Christian Faith.* Amazon/KDP, 2021.

_____ . *Translations of Select Bible Books.* Amazon/KDP 2019.

Ramm, Bernard. *Protestant Biblical Interpretation.* 3rd Revised Edition. Grand Rapids, MI: Baker Book House, 1995.

Roberts, Alexander and James Donaldson. *Ante-Nicene Fathers*, vol. 1, *The Apostolic Fathers, Justin Martyr, Irenaeus.* 1885, Reprinted, Peabody, MA: Hendrickson Publishers, 1995.

Ryrie, Charles C. *Dispensationalism.* Chicago, IL: Moody Press, 1995.

_____ . *The Basis of Premillennial Faith.* Neptune, NJ: Loizeaux Brothers, 1953.

Sproul, R. C. Tabletalk Magazine. *Death Does Not Have the Last Word.* October 1, 2011. Accessed online at Ligonier Ministries: https://www.ligonier.org/learn/articles/death-does-not-have-the-last-word/

Trench, Richard C. *Commentary on the Epistles to the Seven Churches in Asia.* London, 1897.

Vine, W. E. and C. F. Hogg. *Expository Commentary on 1 & 2 Thessalonians.* 1914. Reprinted, Nashville, TN: Thomas Nelson Publishers, 1997.

Waldron, Samuel E. *MacArthur's Millennial Manifesto, A Friendly Response*. Owensboro, KY: Reformed Baptist Academic Press, 2008.

Wallace, Daniel B. *Greek Grammar Beyond the Basics*. Grand Rapids, MI: Zondervan, 1996.

Zodhiates, Spiros. *The Complete Word Study Dictionary New Testament*. Revised. Chattanooga, TN: AMG Publishers, 1993.

www.ingramcontent.com/pod-product-compliance
Lightning Source LLC
Chambersburg PA
CBHW070712130626
46553CB00005B/1955